SpringerBriefs in Population Studies

More information about this series at http://www.springer.com/series/10047

Marina Zannella

The Economic Lifecycle, Gender and Intergenerational Support

National Transfer Accounts for Italy

Springer

Marina Zannella
Department of Methods and Models for Economics, Territory and Finance (MEMOTEF)
Sapienza University of Rome
Rome
Italy

and

Wittgenstein Centre for Demography and Global Human Capital
Vienna Institute of Demography
Vienna
Austria

ISSN 2211-3215 ISSN 2211-3223 (electronic)
SpringerBriefs in Population Studies
ISBN 978-3-319-62667-3 ISBN 978-3-319-62669-7 (eBook)
DOI 10.1007/978-3-319-62669-7

Library of Congress Control Number: 2017946029

Printed on acid-free paper

This Springer imprint is published by Springer Nature
The registered company is Springer International Publishing AG
The registered company address is: Gewerbestrasse 11, 6330 Cham, Switzerland

Acknowledgements

I am grateful to the members of the National Transfer Accounts and of the Agenta project for the stimulating meetings and conversations.

Contents

Abbreviations

AGENTA	Ageing Europe An application of National Transfer Accounts for explaining and projecting trends in public finances. Collaborative project, 7th Framework Programme
COFOG	Classification of the functions of government
COICOP	Individual consumption according to the purpose
ESA	European System of National Accounts
ESSPROSS	European System of Integrated Social Protection Statistics
EU-SILC	European Statistics on Income and Living Conditions
GDP	Gross Domestic Product
HBS	Household Budget Survey
HETUS	Harmonised European Time Use Survey
INPS	Italian National Institute of Social Insurance
Istat	Italian National Institute of Statistics
LCD/LCS	Life cycle deficit/surplus
MTUS	Multinational Time Use Study
NPISH	Households and nonprofit institutions serving households
NTA	National Transfer Accounts
NTTA	National Time Transfer Accounts
SHIW	Survey on Household Income and Wealth
SNA	System of National Accounts
UDB IT-SILC	Italian survey on living conditions

Introduction

How are we to define old age? Can we fix its boundaries in the context of an ever-changing meaning of aging? What are the economic implications of an aging society? How can welfare states deal with aging? Is an aging population sustainable in the long run? These are only some of the questions that arise from changing demographic structures, which in recent years have been receiving increasing attention from scholars, policymakers and society at large. From a demographic perspective, population aging is a combination of increasing longevity and declining fertility that changes the traditional balances in the population age structure; it means not only that many people are living longer, but also that there are fewer children and working age people.

Intergenerational relations are inherently relevant to aging societies and aspects related to their equity and sustainability are becoming a major challenge for contemporary welfare states. A generational contract scenario has been hypothesized by optimists, whereas more pessimistic views predict different alarming futures rife with intergenerational conflict. Regardless of the position taken, the intergenerational debate has focused on the public sector, whereas intergenerational transfers across family members have long been disregarded, due to a lack of information and economic data in this area. Noncash familial transfers in the form of unpaid domestic work have been especially neglected, leading to an undervaluation of women's contribution to the economy. In recent years, the women's movement, the flourishing of comparative welfare literature, and the increasing availability of time use surveys have brought with them a general awareness that "gender matters". The existence of a gender contract has been explicitly recognized not only by scholars but also by institutions at different levels. The societal and demographic changes that have occurred in recent decades call for a rethinking of the generational and the gender contracts on the basis of new social needs and risks.

There have been few attempts to date to analyze the intergenerational reallocation system comprehensively and to integrate the gender perspective into the analysis of intergenerational transfers in a systematic fashion. The National Transfer Accounts (NTA, www.ntaccounts.org) project has worked to fill this gap by developing a methodological framework to measure economic activities throughout the life course and to analyze flows of resources comprehensively between generations and genders. In this monograph, the NTA methodological and conceptual framework is employed to obtain a picture of age- and gender-related economic interactions in Italy during 2008. Chapter 1 provides the book's conceptual background by analyzing different aspects of the generational and gender contracts and their evolution over time. Chapter 2 describes the main data sources and methods used to estimate the economic lifecycle and age reallocation for Italy based on the NTA approach, with the specific aim of making visible the linkage between the NTA global methodology as published by the United Nations, the European NTA methodology recently developed by the project AGENTA (http://www.agenta-project.eu/en/about-agenta.htm), and detailed single-country NTA estimates, taking Italy as a case study. Chapter 3 presents the main results for the economic lifecycle and intergenerational reallocation system for Italy in 2008, based on the NTA, with a focus on the role of both families and the state in financing the consumption of dependent ages. Finally, Chapter 4 extends the analysis of intergenerational economic relations to include gender and the non-market dimensions of the economy by estimating the National Time Transfer Accounts (NTTA). The combination of NTA and NTTA estimates provides us with a much more comprehensive and accurate cross-sectional picture for Italy of age and gender economic activities and transfers.

Chapter 1
The Generational and the Gender Contract

Abstract This chapter presents the conceptual background of this book, aiming to analyze different aspects of the generational and the gender contracts and their evolution over time. Conceptual issues related to the definition of population aging are introduced. An overview of the literature on economic relations and on the direction of transfers between generations is provided. Intergenerational solidarity within families and the state is identified as a fundamental resource in the context of significant demographic and social change. The generational contract is explicitly recognized to be significantly dependent on a gender contract; discussion around women's work for household servicing is thus reported. Finally, the NTA is presented as a method to account for both the quantitative and the behavioral effects of changing demographic structures and to measure and analyze exhaustively intergenerational and gender relations and exchanges in the economy.

1.1 Introduction

Aging has become a key topic in today's societies, attracting wide attention not only from scholars but also from politicians and the media, as shown by the rapidly increasing number of academic studies, technical reports, and newspaper articles appearing in recent years. From a demographic point of view, population aging is the result of a process of declines in both mortality and fertility and the resultant shift in the population age structure. Because mortality and fertility declines have occurred earlier in more developed countries, different nations are at different stages of the aging process. However, population aging is now growing in most low-income countries and will soon become a global phenomenon (United Nations 2015).

Europe moved into the aging process in the 1960s when gains in life expectancy started to appear. These gains were particularly favorable in Italy, where life expectancy at birth increased by more than 11 years from 1960 to 2012. Drops in fertility took place at different times in European countries; it had already dropped below replacement level in the mid-1960s in the Nordic countries. In the UK and

M. Zannella, *The Economic Lifecycle, Gender and Intergenerational Support*, SpringerBriefs in Population Studies, DOI 10.1007/978-3-319-62669-7_1

most continental countries including Italy, fertility declines occurred in the 1970s, while the rest of Europe's Mediterranean nations saw drops in the 1980s (European Commission 2014).[1] Fertility has now recovered in some European countries, especially those where the fall begun earliest, attenuating the aging process. However, fertility remains very low in a number of countries, including Italy, causing rapid and significant population aging. Italy now has the third-highest proportion of older people in the world.

Aging certainly represents a major challenge for all contemporary societies, especially as the process is expected to occur rapidly in low-income countries over the coming decades. Intergenerational relations are a key dimension in the challenges that population aging will pose for the economy and other areas of the society. Efforts to analyze the role of intergenerational relationships in the economy date back to Samuelson's overlapping generations model (1958). However, it is only since the 1990s that the role of the public sector in redistributing resources across generations has been investigated intensively. Scholars have focused largely on aspects related to fiscal sustainability and equity (e.g., Auerbach et al. 1994). The main argument is whether the growing cost of old-age pensions and health care would excessively bias public transfers and overburden the working age population, giving rise to a "generational conflict" (Preston 1984). By contrast, the term "generational contract" has been used to indicate the existence of reciprocal support between generations, either formally through public programs or informally through the family (Bengtson and Achenbaum 1993). Solidarity between generations at all levels—family, community, state—has been universally identified as of crucial relevance in a context of significant demographic and socioeconomic changes (United Nations 2002). However, it has been explicitly recognized that intergenerational solidarity, or the generational contract, relies heavily on the existence of a gender contract, which is defined as the explicit and implicit rules regulating gender relations and the assignment of different work, values, and responsibilities to men and women (European Commission 1998).

Section 1.2 of this chapter introduces the general conceptual issues related to the definition of aging and briefly reviews the literature on economic relations across generations before describing the NTA approach in Sect. 1.3. Section 1.4 analyzes changes in the economic lifecycle in terms of age patterns in consumption and production and examines variations in the direction of intergenerational transfers across different societies. Section 1.5 extends the analysis of intergenerational transfers by considering familial transfers in the form of unpaid time devoted to care and household servicing, along with the more widely recognized financial assistance. Section 1.6 concludes the chapter.

[1]Fertility also fell below replacement levels in the mid-1960s in Luxembourg, Germany, Hungary, (today's) Czech Republic, and Latvia. Drops occurred in the 1980s in Ireland, Malta, Poland, and Slovakia.

1.2 The Meanings of Aging

Aging involves many different aspects of life and societies, ranging from biological and medical issues concerned with extending life expectancy to socioeconomic issues related to changing population structures. However, when it comes to considering aging, we should first define key terms. Age has traditionally been a retrospective concept. Demographic measures refer to chronological age and use conventional age borders such as 60 or 65 years to define the "elderly" or "senior citizens." The specific choice of cutoff age is typically driven by the age of retirement eligibility. Thus, the proportion of people aged 60 or 65 years and older is used to provide measures of population aging at the aggregate population level. Sanderson and Scherbov (2005, 2007) propose "prospective age" as a forward-looking measure of aging based on the number of years left to live. These scholars argue that looking at prospective age is relevant in that many behaviors are influenced by expectations of the remaining part of life to live. D'Albis and Collard (2013) criticize traditional demographic measures based on fixed ages for being non-neutral indicators; they propose an alternative measure of population aging based on the relative age of individuals within a population. Fealy et al. (2012) emphasize the role of public discourse in depicting the elderly, by which "old age" is a social identity constructed through a wide variety of texts ranging from academic studies and policy reports to popular media that give rise to different narratives and public perceptions and are ultimately targeted to particular political or social ends. Their study reveals the existence of a latent ageism—the tendency to propagate negative stereotypes of elderly as dependent and frail—in the public discourse constructing old-age identity.

The different narratives behind the social construction of old age can be divided into more optimistic and more pessimistic views. The latter often predict alarming aging scenarios based on accounting effects, the purely quantitative effects of the changing sizes of different age groups. Typical pessimistic arguments include the negative impact on economic growth of an increasing proportion of older people and a shrinking working age population, the high costs to the state caused by growing life expectancy particularly in expenditures for health and pensions, the boost in political power of older citizens whose sheer numbers will allow them to advance their own social interests, and a significant bias in public expenditure toward older population cohorts and the consequent squeeze of workers' resources, which has serious implications in terms of fiscal sustainability and intergenerational equity. More optimistic views often take into account the role of behavioral changes in response to demographic changes related to population aging, such as longer, fuller lives and smaller families; the accounting and behavioral effects are described in Bloom et al. (2010). Higher life expectancy has been associated with the compression of morbidity and better health conditions (Vaupel 2010). An increase in the savings rate is often cited as an example of a positive behavioral change related to aging. Human capital investment has been proven to be greater in lower rather than higher fertility contexts, with small families devoting more resources to their children, who in turn become more educated and healthier adults who positively influence economic growth (Lee and Mason 2011).

The NTA offers a method to account for both the quantitative and behavioral effects of changing demographic structures by identifying the age borders of economic dependence on the basis of the actual age patterns of consumption and production rather than referring to fixed ages, and to provide an exhaustive measurement and analysis of intergenerational relations and exchanges in the economy. The NTA is meant to complement the UN's System of National Accounts (SNA) with age-specific information on consumption, production, savings, and transfers. Indeed, NTA estimates are constructed so as to be consistent with SNA measures for comparison purposes. The NTA methodology is outlined in Chap. 2, while detailed explanations can be found in United Nations (2013).

1.3 NTA: Key Concepts

The NTA framework is grounded on the key concept of an economic lifecycle, which accounts for the fact that individuals experience systematic changes in their economic behaviors during the life course. People at different ages have different needs and thus consume differently. Individuals at different ages also vary in the ways in which their own consumption is financed (Lee and Mason 2011). In contemporary societies, people during the initial and ending stages of the life course generally do not engage in paid work, so they depend on other people to finance their own consumption or, in NTA terms, they have a lifecycle deficit (LCD) that must be financed through intergenerational transfers and reallocations. On the other hand, people in the middle periods of life produce more on average through labor income than what they consume, generating a surplus that allows for transfers to deficit age groups and, eventually, to savings. Fundamentally, the LCD is determined by the difference between consumption and labor income at each age. A positive value in this difference indicates that consumption falls short of labor income, giving rise to a LCD that must be financed though age reallocations. On the other hand, a negative value indicates that labor income exceeds consumption, generating a lifecycle surplus (LCS) that can be transferred to other individuals or saved.

The LCD can be used to calculate indicators of effective economic dependence within a country. Traditional demographic indicators of economic dependence are based on exogenously fixed age limits; for example, old-age dependency is usually measured as the ratio between the number of persons aged 65 and over and thus considered economically inactive and the number of persons aged between 15 and 64, who are considered economically active. The same logic applies to young-age dependency, with only a numerator change to the number of persons aged 0–14 years or sometimes 0–19 years. Otherwise, the NTA age boundaries for the economic activity or dependence of a population are endogenously determined by age profiles of consumption and labor income. Comparison across European countries has reported that, according to NTA measures, the economic dependence of the young population lasts on average 5 years longer compared to traditional demographic measures that use age 19 as the upper limit for economic inactivity (Hammer et al. 2015). On the other hand, old-age dependency starts about 6 years earlier than the most common traditional cutoff age of 65 years. A support ratio can thus be calculated as the ratio of the effective number of consumers to the effective number of producers. NTA measures such as LCD, LCS, and support ratio offer the great advantage of reflecting country-specific age patterns of production and consumption in addition to the population age structure. The NTA measures economic activity and dependence, thus accounting not only for changes in the population age structure but also for the evolution of economic behaviors during the life course across different times and settings, which is of particular relevance in a general context of the continuously evolving meaning of old age.

By offering a complete and detailed view of intergenerational reallocations and their underlying economic and institutional mechanisms, the NTA approach contributes significantly to broadening our understanding of the generational economy by detailing the ways in which people consume, produce, share, and save resources at different ages as well as the (explicit and implicit) contracts regulating the intergenerational flows of resources (Lee and Mason 2011). There are two main economic mechanisms regulating intergenerational flows of resources: transfers and asset-based reallocations. Intergenerational transfers are flows of resources that do not involve any explicit exchange, while asset-based reallocations can be realized through the use of savings and asset income. Each economic mechanism can be mediated by both the public and private sectors. The latter coincides perfectly almost with the family but also includes institutions such as private charities and nongovernmental organizations. The NTA approach further distinguishes transfers mediated by the family into inter- and intra-household transfers. The quantification of familial transfers is a central and innovative aspect in NTA since, despite their undeniable social and economic relevance, data in this area are lacking.

1.4 The Economic Lifecycle and the Direction of Intergenerational Transfers

The economic lifecycle highlights the existence of common features in all contemporary societies; children and the elderly produce less than what they consume and thus experience economic dependence. Conversely, people in the middle stages of the life course generally produce more by means of their labor than what is needed to fund their own consumption. Behind the existence of these nearly universal patterns, both the shape and intensity of the LCD and LCS vary significantly from setting to setting, according to demographic and institutional characteristics and different underlying macroeconomic situations. In this regard, it is important to note that the economic lifecycle assumes different meanings when we look at per capita versus aggregate age profiles. Per capita age profiles are calculated as age-specific averages for the population and depend on a number of political, cultural, and socioeconomic factors affecting the economic behaviors of individuals. The aggregate economic lifecycle, i.e., averages by age weighted by the corresponding proportion of the population, reflects per capita age profiles of consumption and labor income and the population age structure.

Lee and Mason (2011) reported evidence for higher per capita LCD values during the early stages of life in higher than lower income countries. The difference is explained by a corresponding greater human capital investment in rich, low-fertility countries, particularly in terms of prolonged expenditures for education. Richer countries also show higher per capita values of old-age dependency, due mostly to health expenditures and living-alone arrangements, which carry higher costs than intergenerational co-residence. The LCS shows a reasonably similar pattern, even though labor income peaks earlier and lasts longer in lower than in higher income economies. At the aggregate level, the childhood deficit is larger in poorer than in richer countries, due to the presence of a younger overall population. On the other hand, old-age dependency is becoming increasingly important for rich countries that have reached the later phases of the demographic transition. Differences in the economic lifecycle are not only observed across heterogeneous countries in terms of demographic transition and economic development; a comparative European study has shown that the economic lifecycle also differs across more homogenous countries with regard to the exact age at which the LCD turns positive or negative and to the magnitude of deficits and surpluses (Hammer et al. 2015).

Influential studies have analyzed the directions of transfers in traditional societies. Caldwell (1976) assumed fertility decisions in all societies to be economically rational responses to wealth flow directions that thus play a fundamental role in the demographic transition. According to Caldwell, in primitive and traditional societies transfers flow upward from children to their parents, so high fertility is a rational behavior. As modernization proceeds, the directions of net wealth reverses, becoming downward, and fertility is reduced. However, Kaplan (1994), analyzing data in three different traditional societies, found evidence for a downward direction of transfers in high-fertility settings. In the same fashion, Lee's (2003) comprehensive study of historical changes in demographic structure, welfare, and intergenerational transfers found a downward direction of intergenerational transfers in preindustrial agricultural societies. Lee also presented evidence for an upward direction of net transfers in industrial societies, due primarily to capital accumulation and public reallocations toward older age cohorts, even though transfers within families remain strongly downward.

Recent studies have confirmed the existence of upward and downward patterns of transfers within the state and the family, respectively (Albertini et al. 2007; Albertini and Kohli 2012). This research focused on institutional and cultural factors affecting the magnitude and the direction of familial transfers, with results showing financial transfers through the family are less frequent but more intense in southern compared to Nordic European countries, with continental nations falling between the two extremes. Co-residence appears to play a fundamental role in determining the magnitude and frequency of transfers. In southern European countries, family support is provided through prolonged co-residence and shared consumption, but familial financial support is unlikely to occur once residential autonomy is achieved, and adult children are expected to move back to the parental home when experiencing economic distress. Children in most other continental European countries continue to receive familial support when they become residentially autonomous. In the Nordic countries, children are expected to leave the parental home before concluding their transition to adulthood and thus receive direct financial support.

Overall, NTA research has shown that children's dependency has always existed; this has not always been true of old-age dependency, which is a feature of contemporary societies that results from population aging and changes in the economic lifecycle. Thus, as the demographic transition proceeds, there is a reversal in the direction of intergenerational transfers due to the emergence of a more numerous and more dependent older population (see Lee and Mason 2011). Lee and Donehower (2011) report intra-household transfers to be 90% of private transfers in contemporary societies, ranging from 25% of gross domestic product (GDP) in Western economies to 40% in Southeast Asia. According to the authors, children are on average net beneficiaries of private transfers until they reach their twenties and older people continue to make transfers to younger family members at least into their seventies. Meanwhile, public transfers are a relatively new phenomenon made possible by the rise of the welfare state and the expansion of the public sector in the nineteenth and twentieth centuries. Public transfers vary considerably in magnitude, ranging from 21 to 80% of all transfers among NTA countries (Miller 2011). Public transfers also vary in their trajectories, with rich countries showing the existence of a distinctive upward direction.

1.5 Household Production and Non-market Transfers

After World War II, societies were organized around the Fordist male breadwinner family model; hence, the provision of welfare was sustained by the two main pillars of fathers' paid work and mothers' unpaid care (Esping-Andersen 1999; Lewis 1992; O'Connor 1996). The postwar "housewife contract" (Hirdman 1988) has been eroded by important cultural and societal changes that have occurred since the 1970s, above all the massive participation of women in the labor market. The spread of atypical employment, with its implications in terms of secure income and life course trajectories, also contributed to undermining the foundations of the classic welfare state. Despite the significant increase in female labor market participation over recent decades, women continue to carry out most unpaid work and take most of the responsibility for care within the family (Bianchi et al. 2012).

Unpaid domestic work is invisible in the SNA, so standard economic measures undervalue total production and are particularly biased against women. As early as the first efforts to set standards for national income accounting, the restriction of production to market boundaries was already being questioned. Kuznets (1934) contested the limits of GDP as a measure of a nation's economic well-being and explicitly recognized the economic value of housework as a significant part of the national product, estimating the value of household production to be 26% of GDP for the US in 1929 (Kuznets et al. 1944). Similar attempts were undertaken for Sweden (Lindahl et al. 1937) and the UK (Clark 1958), the respective household productions of which were estimated to represent 32 and 44% of GDP (see Chadeau 1985).

However, it is only since the 1990s that the interrelations between social policies and gender have become a focus of academics and politicians. The flourishing of comparative welfare literature contributed greatly to achieving the recognition that gender matters. Household welfare provision in the form of unpaid work for household self-servicing has now been recognized as a fundamental aspect of the intergenerational support system. In particular, care represents a strong argument for going beyond the traditional emphasis of welfare literature on cash transfers and its relative neglect of the household service dimension. After a period of pressure from the women's movement, the SNA revision (United Nations 1993) suggested the development of satellite accounts for domestic production. This idea was reinforced in 1995 by the United Nations Fourth World Conference on Women's call for national and international statistical organizations to develop time use surveys as a tool to measure unpaid domestic work and estimate its value in satellite accounts. Individual scholars carried out fundamental research to serve as the basis for the development of such accounts (e.g., Goldschmidt-Clermont 1999; Holloway et al. 2002; Ironmonger 1996; Landefeld and McCulla 2000). Ironmonger (1996) proposed developing a measure called the gross economic product as the sum of gross market production and gross household production. A panel was established by the Committee of National Statistics to design non-market satellite accounts for the US; its final findings and recommendations can be found in Abraham and Mackie (2005).

In more recent years, the interest in household production has been extended from the macro- to the micro-level perspective through the development of time use studies. Comparative time use studies analyzing the gender division of labor demonstrate the existence of a significant gender gap in unpaid domestic work during most of the life course, especially in households with young children, which declines only after retirement age (e.g., Anxo et al. 2007; Apps and Rees 2005). These arguments have raised concerns about the existence of a double shift or a dual burden (Hochschild and Machung 1989) and a consequent time squeeze for women (Hochschild 1997; Sayer 2005).

Since 2010, the idea that a full picture of the intergenerational reallocation system could not be obtained without the inclusion of non-market and gender dimensions has gained ground within the NTA project. Thus, the NTA working group on gender, under the guidance of Gretchen Donehower, began to develop methodological approaches in order to disaggregate NTA measures further by gender in addition to age, building on time use surveys to develop a corresponding account for non-market activities, the NTTA. Explanations of the methods used to incorporate gender and time use data in the NTA are reported in Donehower (2014) and United Nations (2013). Combining NTA and NTTA estimates by age and gender provide us with significantly better measures of families' and women's contributions to the actual economy and thus with a more complete picture of the generational and gender contracts.

1.6 Concluding Remarks

Patterns of intergenerational and gender reallocations affect societies in many ways, including fertility choices, human capital formation, and wealth accumulation (Lee and Mason 2011). They can also have a great impact on individuals, influencing their possibilities, behaviors, and choices. Generally, children depend on familial and societal economic transfers both to ensure their survival and to determine their future possibilities through investment in their human capital. However, the timespan of children's economic dependency varies not only in different societies but can also differ in terms of market versus non-market activities. Economic transfers also appear to have an increasing influence on quality of life and well-being during the later stages of life. The intergenerational support system relies heavily on a gender contract; women take most of the responsibility for intergenerational obligations within the family by providing care and unpaid domestic goods and services. The inclusion of gender and the non-market economy was intended as a natural extension of the NTA approach, not only because the generational contract has always depended on a gender contract but also because household service represents a fundamental part of the intergenerational support system.

The analysis of intergenerational transfers represents a fundamental and necessary tool for both policymakers and researchers to understand accurately and address appropriately the consequences of population aging in terms of the equity and sustainability of the welfare system. The societal and demographic changes occurring in recent decades demanded a reconfiguration of the generational and gender contracts on the basis of newly emerging social needs and risks. The urgency of this reconsideration has been reinforced by growing concerns, caused by the recent financial crisis and widespread economic recession, about the sustainability and equity of the existing generational and gender contracts. Although the importance of an in-depth understanding of intergenerational reallocations has now been widely recognized, very few attempts have yet been undertaken to comprehend the underlying institutional and economic mechanisms fully, as studies have focused primarily on specific aspects of the reallocation system. Similarly, efforts to integrate the gender perspective systematically into the analysis of intergenerational transfers by considering both the formal and informal parts of the economy have been lacking. The NTA project seeks to fill this gap; it represents an innovative effort to analyze the flow of resources between generations and genders comprehensively, providing a systematic methodological and conceptual framework with the crucial added value of a comparative international perspective.

References

Abraham, K., & Mackie, C. (2005). *Beyond the market: Designing nonmarket accounts for the United States*. Washington, DC: National Academies Press.

Albertini, M., Kohli, M., & Vogel, C. (2007). Intergenerational transfers of time and money in European families: Common patterns—different regimes? *Journal of European Social Policy, 17*(4), 319–334.

Albertini, M., & Kohli, M. (2012). The generational contract in the family: An analysis of transfer regimes in Europe. *European Social Review, 29*(4), 828–840.

Anxo, D., Mencarini, A., Pailhé, A., Solaz, A., Tanturri, M. L., & Flood, L. (2007). Gender differences in time use over the life course in France, Italy, Sweden, and the US. *Feminist Economics, 17*(3), 159–195.

Apps, P., & Rees, P. (2005). Gender, time use, and public policy over the life cycle. *Oxford Review of Economic Policy, 21*(3), 439–461.

Auerbach, A. J., Gokhale, J., & Kotlikoff, L. J. (1994). Generational accounting: A meaningful way to evaluate fiscal policy. *The Journal of Economic Perspectives, 8*(1), 73–94.

Bengtson, V. L., & Achenbaum, W. A. (Eds.). (1993). *The changing contract across generations*. Piscataway, NJ: Transaction Publishers.

Bianchi, S. M., Sayer, L. C., Milkie, M. A., & Robinson, J. P. (2012). Housework: Who did, does or will do it, and how much does it matter? *Social Forces, 91*(1), 55–63.

Bloom, D. E., Canning, D., & Fink, G. (2010). Implications of population ageing for economic growth. *Oxford Review of Economic Policy, 26*(4), 583–612.

Caldwell, J. C. (1976). Toward a restatement of demographic transition theory. *Population and Development Review, 2*(3/4), 321–366.

Chadeau, A. (1985). Measuring household activities: Some international comparisons. *Review of Income and Wealth, 31*(3), 237–253.

Clark, C. (1958). The economics of house-work. *Bulletin of the Oxford University Institute of Economics & Statistics, 20*(2), 205–211.

D'Albis, H., & Collard, F. (2013). Age groups and the measure of population aging. *Demographic Research, 29*(23), 617–640.

Donehower, G. (2014). Incorporating gender and time use into NTA: National Time Transfer Accounts methodology. http://www.ntaccounts.org/doc/repository/Incorporating%20Gender%20and%20Time%20Use%20into%20NTA,%20Version%203.docx. Accessed December 3, 2016.

Esping-Andersen, G. (1999). *Social foundations of postindustrial economies*. Oxford: Oxford University Press.

European Commission. (1998). *100 words for equality: A glossary of terms on equality between women and men*. Luxembourg: Office for Official Publications of the European Communities.

European Commission. (2014). The 2015 ageing report. Underlying assumption and projection Methodologies. *European Economy*.

Fealy, G., McNamara, M., Treacy, M. P., & LYONS, I. (2012). Constructing ageing and age identities: A case study of newspaper discourses. *Ageing & Society, 32*(1), 85–102.

Goldschmidt-Clermont, L., & Pagnossin-Aligisakis, E. (1999). Households' non-SNA production: labour time, value of labour and of product, and contribution to extended private consumption. *Review of Income and Wealth, 45*(4), 519–529.

Hammer, B., Prskawetz, A., & Freund, I. (2015). Production activities and economic dependency by age and gender in Europe: A cross-country comparison. *The Journal of the Economics of Ageing, 5*, 86–97.
Hirdman, Y. (1988). The gender system–reflections on the social subordination of women. *Kvinnovetenskaplig tidskrift, 3*(3).
Hochschild, A. R. (1997). *The time bind: When work becomes home and home becomes work*. New York: Metropolitan Books.
Hochschild, A. R., & Machung, A. (1989). *The second shift: Working parents and the revolution at home*. New York: Avon Books.
Holloway, S., Short, S., & Tamplin, S. (2002). *Household satellite account (experimental) methodology*. London: ONS.
Ironmonger, D. (1996). Counting outputs, capital inputs and caring labor: Estimating gross household product. *Feminist Economics, 2*(3), 37–64.
Kaplan, H. (1994). Evolutionary and wealth flows theories of fertility: Empirical tests and new models. *Population and Development Review, 20*(4), 753–791.
Kuznets, S. (1934). National income 1929–1932: Letter from the Acting Secretary of Commerce. https://fraser.stlouisfed.org/scribd/?title_id=971&filepath=/files/docs/publications/natincome_1934/19340104_nationalinc.pdf. Accessed December 3, 2016.
Kuznets, S., Epstein, L., & Jenks, E. (1944). *National income and its composition* (Vol. II). New York: National Bureau of Economic Research.
Landefeld, J. S., & McCulla, S. H. (2000). Accounting for nonmarket household production within a national accounts framework. *Review of Income and Wealth, 46*(3), 289–307.
Lee, R. (2003). The demographic transition: Three centuries of fundamental change. *The Journal of Economic Perspectives, 17*(4), 167–190.
Lee, R., & Donehower, G. (2011). Private transfers in comparative perspective. In R. Lee & A. Mason (Eds.), *Population aging and the generational economy: A global perspective* (pp. 107–123). Northampton, MA: Edward Elgar Publishing.
Lee, R., & Mason, A. (2011). *Population aging and the generational economy: A global perspective*. Northampton, MA: Edward Elgar Publishing.
Lewis, J. (1992). Gender and the development of welfare regimes. *Journal of European Social Policy, 2*(3), 159–173.
Lindahl, E., Dahlgren, E., & Kock, K. (1937). *National income of Sweden 1861–1930*, I–II, London.
Miller, T. (2011). The rise of the intergenerational state: Aging and development. In R. Lee & A. Mason (Eds.), *Population aging and the generational economy: A global perspective* (pp. 161–184). Northampton, MA: Edward Elgar Publishing.
O'Connor, J. S. (1996). From women in the welfare state to gendering welfare state regimes. *Current Sociology, 44*(2), 1–130.
Preston, S. H. (1984). Children and the elderly: Divergent paths for America's dependents. *Demography, 21*(4), 435–457.
Samuelson, P. A. (1958). An exact consumption-loan model of interest with or without the social contrivance of money. *The Journal of Political Economy, 66*(6), 467–482.
Sanderson, W. C., & Scherbov, S. (2005). Average remaining lifetimes can increase as human populations age. *Nature, 435*(7043), 811–813.
Sanderson, W. C., & Scherbov, S. (2007). A new perspective on population aging. *Demographic Research, 16*(2), 27–58.
Sayer, L. C. (2005). Gender, time and inequality: Trends in women's and men's paid work, unpaid work and free time. *Social Forces, 84*(1), 285–303.
United Nations. (1993). *A system of national accounts*. New York: United Nations. http://unstats.un.org/unsd/nationalaccount/docs/1993sna.pdf. Accessed December 4, 2016.
United Nations. (2002). *Political declaration and Madrid international plan of action on ageing*. New York: United Nations. http://www.un.org/en/events/pastevents/pdfs/Madrid_plan.pdf. Accessed December 4, 2016.

United Nations. (2013). *National transfer accounts manual: Measuring and analysing the generational economy*. New York: United Nations. http://www.un.org/en/development/desa/population/publications/pdf/development/NTA_Manual_12June2013.pdf. Accessed December 4, 2016.

United Nations, Department of Economic and Social Affairs, Population Division. (2015). World Population Ageing 2015 (ST/ESA/SER.A/390).

Vaupel, J. W. (2010). Biodemography of human ageing. *Nature, 464*(7288), 536–542.

Chapter 2
Crafting Age-Specific National Accounts: National Transfer Accounts Data and Methods for Italy

Abstract This chapter presents the main data sources and methods used to estimate the deficit LCD and age reallocation for Italy in 2008, based on the methodological and conceptual NTA framework. Specifically, it aims to make visible the linkage between the global NTA methodology published by the United Nations, the European NTA methodology developed within the AGENTA project and using Eurostat's harmonized data sources, and detailed single-country NTA estimates referring to Italy as a case study. The use of national data sources has been shown to bring a number of advantages in terms of providing valuable insights at the national level without significantly affecting inter-country comparability. However, this would not be possible without the global NTA manual and the underlying research effort to standardize definitions and methodologies. Meanwhile, the use of a European methodology built on harmonized Eurostat data sources represents a logical step toward the systematic generation of accounts for all European countries.

2.1 Introduction

The NTA has its theoretical roots in foundation research by Samuelson (1958) that paved the way for a flourishing literature on intergenerational transfers. The methodological framework originated in the early 1990s (see Lee 1994a, b). The first version of the NTA manual was made available in 2009 (Mason et al. 2009). The methods have been further developed by a dedicated working group and discussed during numerous meetings and workshops. These efforts have been summarized in a book edited by Lee and Mason (2011) illustrating the methodology, applications to several countries, and new NTA research directions. Finally, an official NTA manual was published by the United Nations (2013). The manual contains detailed conceptual, methodological, and practical explanations.

Today, the NTA project relies on the participation of more than 40 countries on four continents. Since its beginning the project has been co-directed by Ronald Lee and Andrew Mason. The lead institutions are the Center for the Economics and

M. Zannella, *The Economic Lifecycle, Gender and Intergenerational Support*, SpringerBriefs in Population Studies, DOI 10.1007/978-3-319-62669-7_2

Demography of Aging, University of California, Berkeley and the East-West Center at the University of Hawaii at Manoa. As the project has been extended to a growing number of countries, regional centers based at the East-West Center (for Asia), the Economic Commission for Latin America and the Caribbean in Santiago, the African Economic Research Consortium in Nairobi, and the Vienna Institute of Demography have been established. The project is organized into national teams of researchers. Due to the heterogeneity of the countries that participate in the project, specific data sources (and sometimes also specific methods) used by national teams to develop the accounts can vary. Despite the existence of differences in data availability, definitions, and collection, a great deal of effort has been expended in standardizing the methodologies and making the results comparable across NTA countries around the world.

At the European level, the project has received funding for the development of the AGENTA project (http://www.agenta-project.eu/en/index.htm). AGENTA builds on the methodological and research NTA framework to analyze the past and forecast the future of intergenerational transfers in aging European societies. Among the distinctive contributions of AGENTA to NTA research are the development of a harmonized methodology for European countries, thanks to the existence of common data sources, standards, and definitions provided by Eurostat. The methodology describing the standard procedure for generating NTAs for European countries from Eurostat data has been published in a manual freely available at the project website (Istenič et al. 2016).

The NTA methodology can be implemented at different interconnected geographical levels: (i) the UN methodology containing the fundamental concepts, methods, and definitions at the global level; (ii) the harmonized methodology for macro-geographic areas, as in the case of the AGENTA manual for European countries; and (iii) detailed data and methods for country-specific estimates. This chapter describes the general NTA methodology and presents the specific data and methods used for Italy, with the aim of emphasizing the link between the global, European, and country-specific NTA methodologies.

In order to develop the NTA estimates for Italy presented in this volume, harmonized data provided by Eurostat have been used only when no additional information was available from national-level data sources, so the European System of National Accounts (ESA) has been used as the data source for economic macro-aggregates. In many cases, original microdata files produced by Italy's National Institute for Statistics (Istat) and using the framework of European statistics on persons and households have been used. Eurostat regulates and coordinates statistics for the European Union, but it does not collect data directly. Data are collected and prepared at the national level by the statistical authorities of member states and transmitted to Eurostat, which processes and publishes comparable statistics. In the process of harmonizing statistics, part of the original information collected by national statistical offices can be lost, so there are cases in which using the original national data can offer advantages in term of information. For example, the original microdata from the Italian survey on living conditions (abbreviated as UDB IT-SILC below) provided by Istat in the framework of the European Statistics on Income and Living Conditions (EU-SILC) have been used.[1] In the EU-SILC's harmonized data, final ages are aggregated into the 80+ age group, whereas the UDB IT-SILC reports detailed age breakdowns for the elderly component of the population. Therefore, using original data from the UDB IT-SILC allows for more detailed estimates of older age groups up to age 90.[2]

The chapter is structured as follows. Sections 2.2 and 2.3 provide general explanations of the NTA approach. Section 2.2 introduces the LCD, the NTA identity, and the age reallocation system; Sect. 2.3 describes the general procedure implemented to estimate NTA age profiles; and Sect. 2.4 provides an initial insight into the necessary analysis for the economic lifecycle. Later sections offer an explanation of the specific data and methods used to estimate age profiles of the LCD's components: labor income (Sect. 2.5); private consumption (Sect. 2.6) detailed for education (Sect. 2.6.1), health (Sect. 2.6.2) and private consumption other than education and health (Sect. 2.6.3); and public consumption (Sect. 2.7) detailed for education (Sect. 2.7.1), health (Sect. 2.7.2). Sections 2.8 and 2.9 respectively introduce the public and private intergenerational reallocation systems and the specific data and methods used to estimate the age profiles of their components, which consist of public (Sect. 2.8.1) and private transfers (Sects. 2.9.1 and 2.9.2) and public and private asset incomes (Sects. 2.8.2 and 2.9.3). Section 2.10 describes the procedure for smoothing and macro-adjustments. Section 2.11 concludes.

2.2 An Overview of the National Transfer Accounts Approach

The NTA estimates the economic flows occurring across age groups of a country's residents over a calendar year. Estimates of NTA age flows are consistent with the corresponding population totals as reported in the SNA, but the NTA differs from the SNA by referring to individuals rather than institutional sectors as the basic unit of analysis; institutional sectors are treated as intermediaries in economic flows among individuals. The United Nations (2013) offers an exhaustive explanation of NTA concepts and methods.

[1]Microdata were accessed and elaborated at the Istat Laboratory for Elementary Data Analysis (Adele).

[2]Age 90 has been set as the upper limit for detailed analysis in this volume due to the extremely small number of people over 90.

The NTA builds on the following economic identity:

$$\underbrace{C(x) - Y^{l}(x)}_{LCD\ or\ LCS} = \underbrace{\tau^{+}(x) - \tau^{-}(x)}_{Transfers} + \underbrace{Y^{A}(x) - S(x)}_{\substack{Asset-based\\ reallocations}}, \tag{2.1}$$

where C is the consumption, Y^{l} is the labor income, Y^{A} is the asset income, S is the savings, and τ^{+} and τ^{-} are the transfers received and paid through the public and the private sector at each age x.

The NTA identity holds in both per capita and aggregate terms, includes both the public and private sectors, and can be detailed for the most relevant age-related portions of consumption and reallocation, such as health, education, or pensions.

The left side of the economic identity represents the LCD or LCS given by the difference between public and private consumptions and labor income by age. A positive difference indicates the existence of an LCD, meaning that consumption falls short of labor income and must be financed through public and private reallocations. A negative difference indicates an LCS, which occurs when labor income exceeds consumption and thus can be saved or transferred to other individuals through the family, the state, or both.

In per capita terms, the economic lifecycle is determined by the interaction of contextual and behavioral factors affecting the relationship between ages on the one hand and consumption and labor income on the other. At the aggregate level, the economic lifecycle reflects both the population age structure and the per capita age profiles.

The right side of the identity represents the intergenerational reallocation system consisting of transfers and asset-based reallocations. Transfers consist of economic flows that do not involve exchange transactions (the explicit exchange of goods and services). Asset-based reallocations consist of asset income that is not saved, where asset income is income from capital and property, including interest payments, dividends, and the rental value of use of a home belonging to the occupant. Asset-based reallocations are inter-temporal exchanges; resources acquired in the past can be used to finance current consumption or saved for the future. Both transfers and reallocations shift resources from surplus ages to deficit ages through the public and private sectors.

The public sector is represented by the state, which in the NTA is an intermediary that realizes intergenerational reallocations by providing services like public programs for education, health, and pensions and goods such as security, receiving taxes, and accumulating public assets and liabilities (saving) or debt (dis-saving). The private sector is represented by households and nonprofit institutions serving households (NPISH) and realizes intergenerational reallocation mainly through cash transfers,[3] accumulation of assets, or savings. However, the vast majority of

[3]According to the SNA, capital transfers (such as bequests and similar large transfers) are not current transfers and are thus not included in the NTA flow account. However, research is

private transfers are mediated by households. Transfers are further distinguished by those taking place among members of the same household (intra-household transfers) and between members of different households (inter-household transfers).

2.3 National Transfer Accounts Age Profiles

Constructing the NTA requires age-specific information on a number of economic activities: age profiles of public and private consumptions, labor income, public and private transfers inflows received and outflows paid, public and private savings, and asset income. However, economic data are only available from the SNA in the form of population aggregates; there is no information on how the economic aggregates break down by age. The NTA seeks to fill this information gap by developing a satellite account for and with age-specific economic data. NTA age profiles are thought to be consistent with the corresponding macro-aggregates in the SNA, with one main exception; private household transfers are not recorded in the SNA. However, transfers occurring within and/or between households represent a fundamental resource in the intergenerational reallocation system and are an essential aspect of the generational economy. The NTA also complements the SNA by providing measures of transfers occurring at the household level.

Estimating age profiles is a fairly complex process that involves the following steps for each economic activity being considered:

1. Identify macro-aggregate values in the SNA;
2. Find the most appropriate available information to distribute macro-aggregates by age. Age proxy information can consist of administrative data or micro-level survey data;
3. Individuate a proper age allocation criterion on the basis of the available age information and the nature of the specific activity. Age allocation criteria consist of equivalence scales that can be found in the literature or inferred through data;
4. Make preliminary estimates of per capita and aggregate age profiles. Aggregate age profiles are obtained as the product between per capita age profiles and the corresponding population size;
5. Smooth age profiles, if necessary (explanations in this regard are reported in Sect. 2.10);
6. Prepare final estimates of per capita and aggregate age profiles. Age profiles are adjusted using a multiplicative factor to ensure their consistency with SNA measures, so that the sum over all age groups equals the corresponding aggregate in the SNA.

(Footnote 3 continued)

currently underway within the NTA project to construct wealth accounts that incorporate capital transfers.

Building the NTA requires extensive data collecting from multiple sources and in-depth analysis of available information together with the use of appropriate calculation methods. In particular, an important aspect of the methodology consists of mapping from the SNA classification of economic variables onto the NTA classification system to ensure correspondence between the two accounts. Macro-aggregates for European countries can be found in the ESA (Eurostat 2013) and are accessible through Eurostat; more details are available in the AGENTA manual (Istenič et al 2016). The choice of 2008 as the reference year for the estimates was motivated by the need to combine different data sources while using the most recent homogeneous data available.

2.4 The Economic Lifecycle

As noted above, the NTA estimates the LCD by comparing age profiles of public and private consumptions and labor income. Macro-aggregates of consumption and labor income are found in sector accounts (Eurostat 2008a), which are published within the annual national accounts. Sector accounts consist of a systematic description of the economic activities by institutional sector. Institutional sectors are institutional units with similar characteristics and behaviors: households and NPISH, nonfinancial corporations, financial corporations, general government, and the rest of the world.

To take into account the different nature of consumption activities, the NTA distinguishes between three main categories: education, health, and consumption other than education and health. The first two are age-sensitive activities and the third is a residual category that includes all remaining types of consumption activities. Macro-aggregates for the three categories are found in the Final Consumption Expenditure of Households by Consumption Purpose (Eurostat 2008b) and the general government expenditure by function (Eurostat 2008c) for private and public consumption, respectively. Eurostat's classifications of private and public consumptions by purpose and function follow the SNA classifications (United Nations 2000)[4] of individual consumption according to the purpose (COICOP) and classification of the functions of government (COFOG).

Table 2.1 provides an initial insight into the anticipated results and the necessary analysis for the economic lifecycle. As shown, macro-aggregate values are obtained from the SNA (except for the LCD, the aggregate of which must be estimated as the difference between consumption and production by age) and must be disaggregated into single-year age groups from ages 0 to age 89, with age 90 including anyone

[4]This classification was approved by the United Nations Statistical Commission in May 1999. A previous version of the classification, known as the functional classification, was included in the 1993 version of the SNA.

Table 2.1 LCD, values at current prices, Italy 2008

LCD and its components	€ (Millions)	Age				
		0	…	*x*	…	90+
LCD	**259,521**					
Consumption	**1,089,769**					
Public consumption	315,406					
Education	*60,661*					
Health	*108,330*					
Other	*146,415*					
Private consumption	774,363					
Education	*7169*					
Health	*22,417*					
Other	*744,777*					
Labor income	**830,248**					
Earnings	680,279					
Self-employment	149,969					

Source Author's elaboration on Eurostat data (Eurostat 2008a, b, c)

older than 90. The methods and data used to disaggregate SNA totals by age are described in detail in subsequent sections of this chapter.

2.5 Labor Income

Labor income consists of paid wages and self-employment, corresponding to the following components of SNA: compensation of employees, labor's share of taxes less subsidies on production, and labor's share of mixed income. Aggregates are reported in Table 2.3 in the Appendix.

Compensation of employees encompasses all compensation for work, including employee cash income, employee noncash income, and employers' social insurance contributions. Cash income refers to the monetary component of the compensation of employees and consists of wages, salaries, and employers' social contributions (the value of taxes paid to the government on behalf of employees). Noncash employee income refers to benefits, such as a company car and associated costs, free or subsidized meals, etc.

Self-employment labor income consists of the portion of gross mixed income in return for labor, while the remaining share of entrepreneurial income is designated as a return to capital. Labor's share of mixed income is not reported in the SNA and hence must be estimated. The NTA, in the absence of information to the contrary, assumes two-thirds of mixed income to be labor income.

Labor income age profiles are based on living condition survey microdata from Istat (Indagine sulle condizioni di vita, 2009). The UDB IT-SILC microdata are part of the EU-SILC. As noted above, original Italian microdata have been used in order to obtain estimates for advanced ages up to 90 years and above. The UDB IT-SILC data come from a survey panel conducted annually on a nationally representative random sample of around 26,000 households and 70,000 individuals distributed across 800 municipalities in Italy. The survey aims to collect timely and comparable cross-sectional and longitudinal microdata on income, poverty, social exclusion, and living conditions. Information on social exclusion and housing conditions is collected at the household level, whereas labor, education, and health information are collected at the individual level for those aged 16 and above. Age profiles of labor income and its main components can be calculated directly from the microdata as individual averages by age.

2.6 Private Consumption

Macro-aggregate values of expenditures divided into education, health, and other private consumption expenditures are found in Eurostat in the Final Consumption Expenditure of Households by Consumption Purpose (Table 2.4 in the Appendix). The economic aggregate of consumption classified by purpose differs from that of total private consumption as reported in the sector accounts, because COICOP private consumption expenditures are adjusted with a multiplicative factor.

The Household Budget Survey (HBS; Istat, Indagine sui Consumi delle famiglie 2008a) is used as proxy information to allocate private consumption by age. HBS is a nationally representative survey focusing on household expenditures on goods and services. Most EU countries launched an HBS at the beginning of the 1960s; Eurostat has collected and published them every 5 years since 1988. Although there have been continuous efforts toward harmonization, differences across countries regarding frequency, timing, contents, and structure of the survey remain. The Italian HBS sample for 2008 has a two-level structure. The primary level consists of approximately 470 municipalities, randomly selected and proportional to their demographic size, that represent the whole country; the second level consists in approximately 28,000 randomly selected households. HBS provides information regarding household consumption expenditures on goods and services, with considerable detail in terms of expenditure categories and including many demographic and socioeconomic characteristics. The HBS is a fundamental tool that is valuable for describing, analyzing, and interpreting the spending behavior of resident households. Data on expenditures are collected at the household level, whereas socio-demographic data are collected at the individual level for household members. Thus, estimates of age profiles of private consumption pose an additional challenge; the age schedule of the economic activity cannot be observed at the individual level, as it can for labor income estimates, meaning that aggregate data at the household level must be allocated to individuals according to their ages. The age criteria for this allocation vary according to the nature of the expenditure and are described in the following subsections.

2.6.1 *Private Education Consumption*

Private education consumption includes books, school supplies (for all levels including pre-school), tutoring expenses, tuition and fees, and all other household expenditures related to education. In the NTA methodology (United Nations 2013), the following linear model is used to assign private education consumption to household members according to age:

$$\mathrm{CFE}_j = \sum_{X=0}^{90+} \alpha(x) \cdot E_j(x) + \varepsilon_j \quad \text{with } \alpha(x) \geq 0, \tag{2.2}$$

where CFE_j is the private education consumption of household j, $E_j(x)$ is the number of enrolled members aged x in household j,[5] and $\alpha(x)$ are the parameters to be estimated. Parameter estimates $\hat{\alpha}(x)$ obtained through the least squares criterion are used to redistribute the education consumption of each household j to the E_j number of household components enrolled in an education program by age x. In other words, parameter estimates can be considered the weights of a data-driven equivalence scale:

$$\mathrm{CFE}_j(x) = \left[\hat{\alpha}(x) \cdot E_j(x)\right] \frac{\mathrm{CFE}_j}{\sum_{X=0}^{90+} \hat{\alpha}(x) \cdot E_j(x)}. \tag{2.3}$$

2.6.2 *Private Health Consumption*

Private health consumption includes out-pocket health expenditures, employer provision of medical services to employees, and reimbursements to health providers by private health insurance companies. Methods to estimate age profiles of private consumption vary across countries due to differences in data availability (see United Nations 2013). In principle, having information about the recipients of expenditures within the household would allow private health consumption to be assigned to household members according to age, similar to education:

[5]Enrolled members are students receiving formal education or those enrolled in other education programs. Information about enrolled members is available in the HBS.

$$\mathrm{CFH}_j = \sum_{x=0}^{90+} \beta(x) \cdot N_j(x) + \varepsilon_j \quad \text{with } \beta(x) \geq 0, \tag{2.4}$$

where CFH_j is the private health consumption for household j, $N_j(x)$ is the number of household j members aged x, and $\beta(x)$ are the parameters to be estimated. However, the Italian data, like most household expenditure surveys, do not report utilization measures for health spending. Therefore, the regression approach has one important limitation; while on the one hand the number of enrolled household members by age represents a reliable variable to identify which individuals in the household benefit from this particular household expenditure; in the case of private health consumption there is no information to capture in order to assign individuals to which the expense should be attributed. As a consequence, the model yields negative parameter estimates and significant standard errors for some age groups.

For the reason explained above, an alternative approach consisting of an iterative proportional fitting procedure (IPFP) has been implemented. The IPFP was originally designed by Deming and Stephan (1940) for the adjustment of frequencies in contingency tables. Later, the IPFP was applied to several statistical problems in different domains. In our case, knowing for each sampled household the age distribution of its components and its expenditures on health allows for health consumption by age to be estimated, subject to the following constraints: (i) total consumption of members of household j must be equal to the expenditure incurred by the household j; and (ii) per capita values of consumption by age do not vary across households.

In a first step, the IPFP assigns health expenditures equally to each household member:

$$\hat{\mathrm{CFH}}_j^1(x) = \mathrm{CFH}_j \frac{N_j(x)}{\sum_{x=0}^{90+} N_j(x)}. \tag{2.5}$$

Based on this preliminary allocation, per capita age profiles are estimated:

$$\hat{\mathrm{PFH}}_j^1(x) = \frac{\sum_{j=1}^{n} \hat{\mathrm{CFH}}_j^1(x) \cdot w_j}{\sum_{j=1}^{n} N_j(x) \cdot w_j} = \frac{\hat{\mathrm{CFH}}^1(x)}{\hat{N}(x)}, \tag{2.6}$$

where n is the sample household size and w_j is the sample weight for the household j.

In the next step, expenditure is allocated proportionally to the per capita age profiles previously obtained:

$$\mathrm{CFH}_j^2(x) = \mathrm{CFH}_j \frac{\hat{\mathrm{PFH}}^1(x) \cdot N_j(x)}{\sum_{x=0}^{90+} \hat{\mathrm{PFH}}^1(x) \cdot N_j(x)}. \tag{2.7}$$

Once again, the values obtained are used for new estimates of per capita age profiles:

$$\hat{\mathrm{PFH}}_j^2(x) = \frac{\sum_{j=1}^{n} \hat{\mathrm{CFH}}_j^2(x) \cdot w_j}{\sum_{j=1}^{n} N_j(x) \cdot w_j} = \frac{\hat{\mathrm{CFH}}^2(x)}{\hat{N}(x)}. \quad (2.8)$$

The procedure is repeated until the maximum difference between the per capita age profiles of two successive steps is lower or equal to a predetermined value δ (with $\delta = 1$ euro).

2.6.3 *Private Consumption Other Than Education and Health*

Other private consumption is a residual category that includes all expenditures not designated for education and health. Other household consumption is allocated using an ad hoc equivalent scale suggested by the NTA and based on an extended review of the existing literature on household consumption. More specifically, the NTA allocates household consumption to household members proportionally to a scale with a constant value equal to 0.4 for children aged 0–4 years, a linearly increasing value from 5 to 19 years, and a value of 1 for 20 years of age and older. The values of the equivalence scale do not vary across households or across countries. However, age profiles of consumption do vary as a result of differences in total household consumption and household composition, along with the interaction between the two (United Nations 2013). Therefore, with CFO_j as other private consumption for household j, $N_j(x)$ as the number of household members aged x, and $\gamma(x)$ as the value of the equivalence scale at age x, other consumption is allocated as follows:

$$\mathrm{CFO}_j(x) = [\gamma(x) \cdot N_j(x)] \frac{\mathrm{CFO}_j}{\sum_{x=0}^{90+} \gamma(x) \cdot N_j(x)}. \quad (2.9)$$

2.7 Public Consumption

Public consumption is the value of goods and services received by individuals from the public sector. Aggregate NTA public consumption finds its SNA counterpart in general government final consumption expenditures, according to which public consumption can be divided into collective and individual expenditures. Collective expenditures are typically those for general public services such as defense, public order and safety, economic affairs, environmental protection, etc.; examples of individual services include education, health, and social protection (Eurostat 2011).

Collective expenditures are public goods that benefit all the members of a population independent of their individual characteristics. Thus, in the NTA logic, the value of public collective consumption is distributed equally among individuals regardless of age. On the other hand, individual expenditures are targeted to individuals with specific characteristics and hence can be allocated by age.

As for private consumption, the NTA considers three categories of public consumption: education, health, and public consumption other than education and health. Aggregate values of general government final expenditures by function are reported in Table 2.5 in the appendix. The most important expenditure category is health, which represents 34.4% of total public consumption, followed by education (19.2%). Collective consumption (composed of general public services, defense, public order and safety, economic affairs, environment protection, housing, and community amenities) accounts for around 39.9% of total public consumption. Therefore, individual consumption (i.e., health, recreation, culture and religion, education, and social protection) represents the majority of public consumption (60.1%). The data and methods used to distribute public consumption for education and health are described in the following subsections.

2.7.1 Public Education Consumption

Public consumption for education refers to government expenditures for the provision of formal and informal education in the form of services provided both to individuals and on a collective basis; examples of the latter include research and development and nonclassified educational expenditures. Formal education expenditures are defined as government spending on primary, secondary, and higher education levels; informal education refers to expenditure on culture, religious studies, and other types of education. Individual consumption represents 95.1% of public expenditure for formal education, whereas the remaining 4.9% is allocated to collective services including research and development receiving 0.1% of education public spending (see Table 2.6 in the Appendix). Among individual expenditures, 50.2% is for secondary education, 37.0% is for pre-primary and primary education, and much less (6.7%) is for post-secondary education, of which 5.4% is for tertiary education and 1.3% for non-tertiary post-secondary education. Public informal and collective education expenditure is not targeted to particular groups and thus is allocated equally to the consumption of each individual. By contrast, public spending for formal education at the individual level benefits only the students enrolled in formal programs and can thus be allocated to the consumption of individuals by age, according to the following equation:

$$\mathrm{CGE}(x) = \sum_i E_i(x) \cdot c_i, \tag{2.10}$$

where i is the educational level, c_i is the unit cost per student at the i educational level, and E_i is the number of students at the i educational level. Unit cost per student at each level of education is calculated as the ratio between public spending on education for the educational level i by the corresponding number of enrolled students. The unit cost of education within each level is assumed not to vary by age; for example, the cost of a 14-year-old high school student is equal to that for a 17-year-old high school student.

The information on the number of enrolled students by age for each educational level is found in administrative data from the Italian Ministry of Education, Universities and Research. This information is generally available by single-year age groups with some exceptions for which the number of students has been estimated on the basis of UDB IT-SILC microdata (Istat 2009).[6]

2.7.2 Public Health Consumption

Public health consumption consists of health care provided by the government directly to individuals, health care purchased by individuals and reimbursed through public programs, and collective services like health education and preventative programs. Table 2.7 in the Appendix reports public health consumption by COFOG group in absolute and relative terms. Classes of expenditure are also shown for each COFOG group. However, macro-aggregates for classes are not reported in that table, since Eurostat's database does not provide economic data at that level of detail.

As with education, health consumption includes expenditures on services provided on both individual and collective bases. Expenditures on individual services correspond to groups 7.1–7.3 in Table 2.7 whereas those for collective services correspond to groups 7.4–7.6. Individual services represent 97.8% of total government spending on health consumption. The largest categories of expenditure are hospital services (56.1%), outpatient services (30.4%), and medical products, appliances, and equipment (11.3%). Collective public health expenditures are not targeted to any specific group and hence are allocated in equal shares to the consumption of individuals. Conversely, government spending for health at the individual level is targeted to users whose age can vary significantly depending on the nature of the expenditure in question.

Ideally, health care provided directly by the government to individuals should be allocated to the consumption of individuals on the basis of administrative records (United Nations 2013). However, administrative data are not always available. At the European level, there is no administrative source providing comparable data on

[6]See Sect. 2.6 for a description of EU-SILC survey.

Table 2.2 Pharmaceutical products' equivalence scale by age groups and gender

Age groups	Males	Females	Total
0	0.73	0.73	0.73
1–4	0.73	0.73	0.73
5–14	0.38	0.38	0.38
15–44	0.47	0.71	0.59
45–64	1.20	1.20	1.20
65–74	1.96	1.96	1.96
75 and older	2.33	2.33	2.33

Source Agenzia Italiana del Farmaco (2010)

government spending for public health[7] (Istenǐc et al. 2016). In the case of Italy, after an extensive review of the available information and data sources, macro-aggregates have been allocated to age by relying on information reported by the Ministry of Economy and Finance (Ministero dell'Economia e delle Finanze 2009) on the prevalent class of expenditure within the corresponding COFOG group. As for public consumption of medical products, appliances, and equipment (group 7.1 in Table 2.7), the main class of expenditure is represented by pharmaceutical products (class 2.1.1). The Italian Medicines Agency (Agenzia Italiana del Farmaco Agenzia Italiana del Farmaco 2010) has calculated an equivalence scale for the consumption of pharmaceutical products by age and gender (the values of the equivalence scale are reported in Table 2.2). Expenditures for the COFOG group in Table 2.7 are allocated to consumption by age, proportionally to values of the equivalence scales.

General and specialized medical services (classes 7.2.1 and 7.2.2) are the principal classes of expenditure for outpatient services (group 7.2). The per capita values of general medical services expenditures by age are determined at the national level in Italy for 2008 as follows: €56.70 for children aged 0–13 years, €38.62 for adults aged 14–78 years, and €54.11 for people aged 75 years and older. Hence, per capita values have been used to redistribute the expenditures on general medical services (7.2.1) by age. Meanwhile specialized medical services (7.2.2) have been attributed to consumption by age by relying on information from microdata on the health status of the population and the use of health services (Istat 2008b), a nationally representative survey carried out approximately once every 5 years with a sample of more than 50,000 households and 128,000 individuals distributed across 1465 municipalities in Italy.

Public expenditures for hospital services have been allocated to consumption by age on the basis of administrative data published in the annual report on hospital discharges (Ministero della Salute 2008) and microdata from Istat (2008b). The Ministry of Health provides data on the number of hospitalizations and the mean cost of hospitalization by 5-year age groups (Table 2.8 in the Appendix), with two

[7]The AGENTA project has been provided by the Aging Working Group (AWG) with pre-calculated age profiles of public health and long-term care consumption.

exceptions: the youngest age group (infants up to one year of age) and the oldest age group (75 years and over). The number of hospitalizations by single-year age groups has been calculated using survey microdata. The cost of hospitalization by single-year age group has been obtained by finding the product between the corresponding number of hospitalizations estimated through microdata and the mean cost of hospitalization reported by the Ministry, which is assumed not to vary by age within a given age group.

In general, age profiles of individual public health consumption suffer from a certain degree of approximation due to difficulties in accessing detailed data, especially those regarded as sensitive by governmental bodies. In the context of increasing longevity, it would be valuable to obtain more detailed estimates of public health expenditures for individuals at older ages, for which access to administrative data on hospital discharges would be needed.

2.8 The Public Intergenerational Reallocation System

Public transfers are current resource flows mediated by the government and implemented through laws and regulations at different administrative levels. Transfers consist of inflows to program beneficiaries and of outflows from taxpayers to fund those programs. If outflows are not sufficient to finance inflows, there is a transfer deficit that can be made up in two ways. Public asset income can be used to finance the public transfer deficit, giving rise to public asset-based reallocations. The other possibility takes place when asset income is insufficient to offset the transfer deficit, so that transfer programs must be financed partly through taking on public debt. In both cases there is an inflow for residents and an outflow for government. Conversely, if net public transfers are positive, there is a transfer surplus resulting from an excess of taxes over transferred public goods and services. In that case, the surplus is saved, generating an inflow for government and an outflow for households.

2.8.1 Public Transfers

Aggregate values of public transfer inflows are provided by Eurostat (2008d) in the European System of Integrated Social Protection Statistics (ESSPROS) and reported in Table 2.9 in the Appendix. Given that pensions represent the great majority of government spending on social protection, Table 2.9 distinguishes broadly between pensions and "other social protection" as a residual category. Aggregate values for social protection functions other than pensions are reported in Table 2.10 in the Appendix. ESSPROS was jointly developed in the late 1970s by Eurostat and EU member states in response to the need for a specific instrument of statistical observation of social protection and in response to the second article of the 1957 Treaty of Rome, which recognizes the promotion of high levels of social protection and the development of the economic and social cohesion of EU states as a priority. The first ESPROSS methodology was published in 1993; it was revised in 1996 and last updated in 2008 (Eurostat 2008e).

ESSPROSS defines social protection as all interventions intended to relieve individuals or households of the burden of a defined set of risks or needs: sickness and health care, disability, old age,[8] survivors, family and children, unemployment, housing, and social exclusion not otherwise enumerated. These various risks or needs define the primary purpose for which resources and benefits are provided and identify the functions of social protection. Public transfer inflows can be provided in cash or in-kind, accounting for 52.3 and 47.7% respectively of total expenditures in this area. In-kind public transfers correspond to public consumption and, similarly, are divided into education, healthcare, and public consumption other than education and health. Thus, the macro-aggregate value of in-kind public transfers is equal to that of public consumption (see Sect. 2.5). Cash public transfers refer to payments received through the social protection system, such as pensions and subsides.

Table 2.9 in the Appendix shows that social protection represents the largest public transfer inflow (46.7% of total inflows), followed by other public transfers (23.9%), health care (19.3%), and education (10.1%). Pensions in turn make up the vast majority of social protection spending, the remainder of which is composed of 44.3% for survivors, 27.4% for disability, 18.3% for families and children, 9.1% for unemployment, and 0.9% for other social exclusion (see Table 2.10 in the Appendix). Unlike other European countries, Italy's social protection expenditures for housing are absent.

Age profiles of in-kind public transfer inflows are equal to those of public consumption for the corresponding government function (see Tables 2.5 and 2.9). Age profiles of cash inflows have been estimated on the basis of administrative data from Italy's Istituto Nazionale della Previdenza Sociale (INPS) analyzed and published in collaboration with Istat, and UDB IT-SILC microdata. INPS-Istat data are provided in 5-year age groups, while EU-SILC microdata have been used to estimate single-year age profiles.

Public transfer outflows can be divided into three main categories: taxes on goods and services; taxes on income, profits, and capital gains; and social contributions. Age profiles of taxes on goods and services are based on those of private transfers, which in turn build on microdata from the HBS. Age profiles of taxes on income and social contributions are estimated with UDB IT-SILC microdata (Istat 2009), whereas microdata from the Survey on Household Income and Wealth

[8]The old age function consists of pensions (including anticipated old age pensions and partial pensions), care allowances other than medical care, and other cash benefits and benefits in-kind such as accommodation and assistance in carrying out daily tasks.

(SHIW; Banca d'Italia, Indagine sui bilanci delle famiglie italiane 2008) are used to estimate age profiles of taxes on income, profits, and capital gains.

The SHIW was initiated in the 1960s with the aim of collecting data on incomes and savings in Italian households. Over the years, the aim of the survey has been expanded to include wealth and other aspects related to households' economic and financial behavior. Until 1987, the survey was conducted with time-independent samples (cross sections) of households. In order to facilitate the analysis of changes in the phenomena being investigated, since 1989 part of the sample has comprised households interviewed in previous surveys, known as panel households. Beginning in 2010, SHIW has provided data on Italy to the Eurosystem's Household Finance and Consumption Survey, which is coordinated by the European Central Bank. The survey sample for 2008 consists of about 8,000 households and 20,000 individuals, selected in two stages, with municipalities and households as the primary and secondary sampling units respectively. Data are collected at both the household and individual levels. Information on the distribution of asset income and savings is reported at the individual level, so age averages can be directly calculated from SHIW microdata.

The use of the SHIW for the estimates of age profiles of savings and asset income represents a further example of the informational advantages that can be derived by the use of national data sources. In the framework of the harmonized NTA methodology for European countries, estimates of the age profiles of taxes on asset income, profits, and capital gains build on a number of variables from EU-SILC that are only provided at the household level (see Istenič et al. 2016). In order to estimate the age profiles, the value of these variables is assumed to be assigned entirely to the head of household, but the use of this assumption is not necessary for Italy, where individual SHIW data on savings and asset income allow for direct estimates of the corresponding age-specific averages.

2.8.2 Public Asset-Based Reallocations

Table 2.11 in the Appendix shows the mechanisms underlying the public reallocation system. As explained in Sect. 2.7, asset-based reallocations are a balancing item between public transfer outflows and inflows. Therefore, public asset reallocations are equal to the transfer deficit or surplus. Public asset reallocations consist of two flows: public asset income and savings. Public asset reallocations are given by the difference between asset income and savings. Public asset income and savings are allocated to age according to the age profiles of taxpayers, so age profiles of public asset reallocations are estimated using the same procedure followed for allocating public transfer outflows.

2.9 The Private Intergenerational Reallocation System

The NTA considers two kinds of private intergenerational transfers, inter-household and intra-household. Inter-household transfers occur between different households and are mediated by households or NPISH; intra-household transfers occur within the same household between members of that household. As detailed in the following subsections, macro-aggregates for private transfers are not available from the SNA or any other official data source and must be estimated indirectly, whereas macro-aggregates for inter-household transfers can be estimated from the limited information available from survey microdata. The quantification of private transfers represents a major contribution of the NTA to detailing national accounts and the development of welfare measures.

2.9.1 Inter-household Transfers

Inter-household transfer aggregates are calculated using UDB IT-SILC microdata (Istat 2009). UDB IT-SILC microdata contain information on the amount of regular inter-household cash transfers paid (outflows) and received (inflows). In a closed economy, total inter-household transfer inflows must equal outflows. However, inflows and outflows can differ due to flows to and from the rest of the world. Therefore, population aggregates for inter-household inflows and outflows based on UDB IT-SILC are adjusted to ensure their consistency with the aggregate net flows to the rest of the world reported in the SNA.

In the NTA framework, inter-household transfers are assigned to heads of households, given that in most cases no information is available at the individual level, which is also true of the Eurostat data source reported by Istenič et al. (2016). Therefore, age profiles of inter-household transfer inflows and outflows are estimated by tabulating sample values using the age of heads of households. The main reason for the adoption of this age criterion is that the general absence of information in this regard does not allow for reliable assumptions on the direction of flows, especially considering the heterogeneity of NTA countries and the need to ensure comparability of the results. However, this age allocation criterion has long been debated within the NTA project due to a major conceptual limitation: the age profiles depend on the definition of head of household and may not reflect the actual age directions of the flows. Once again, the use of original national data sources represents an advantage in terms of information: the Italian UDB IT-SILC exceptionally provides information about inter-household transfers paid and received by household members. Thus, age profiles for inter-household transfers have been directly calculated on the basis of UDB IT-SILC microdata.

2.9.2 Intra-household Transfers

As noted above, due to a lack of data, population aggregates for intra-household transfers are estimated indirectly as the balancing item between private consumption and disposable income at each age.

Computing intra-household transfers requires extensive data preparation. The estimates require two kinds of data: a nationally representative household survey that provides information about household features such as number of members and socio-demographic characteristics like gender, age, family relation, etc., and previously estimated per capita age profiles. UDB IT-SILC microdata were used as the representative household survey, because they are based on a nationally representative sample of sufficient size (20,928 households and 52,433 individuals) to provide a reliable estimate of the socio-demographic structure of Italian families. Through that microdata, an initial data set containing the following variables was created: identification codes for households and household members, age, relationship to head of household, and sample weights. Then, a second data set was created, containing the previously estimated per capita age profiles of labor income, current private consumption, durable private consumption, net inter-household transfers, public cash transfer inflows, and taxes paid. Linking the two data sets makes it possible to associate the appropriate per capita age profile with each household member in the sample. This led to the creation of a third data set, containing the following variables for each individual i in the household j:

$x(j, i)$ = age of the household member i in the household j;
head(j, i) is 1 if the household member i is the household head; otherwise is 0;
YL(j, i) is the labor income;
CFC(j, i) is the current private consumption;
TGCI(j, i) is the public cash transfer inflows;
TGT(j, i) is the taxes paid;
TFB(j, i) is the net inter-household transfers; and
$w(j, i)$ is the sample weight.

Estimating per capita age profiles of intra-household transfers is a fairly complex process that requires five main steps. The first consists of computing the deficit or surplus, given by the difference between disposable income and private consumption, for each member i of the household j. Disposable income (YD) is equal to labor income plus public cash transfer inflows plus net inter-household transfers, less taxes paid:

$$\mathrm{YD}(j,i) = \mathrm{YL}(j,i) + \mathrm{TGCI}(j,i) + \mathrm{TFB}(j,i) - \mathrm{TGT}(j,i). \tag{2.11}$$

If disposable income exceeds consumption, the member i of the household j has a surplus defined in the equation as SUR:

$$\mathrm{SUR}(j,i) = \mathrm{YD}(j,i) - \mathrm{CFC}(j,i). \tag{2.12}$$

Conversely, if consumption exceeds disposable income, the member i of the household j has a deficit (DEF) given by

$$\mathrm{DEF}(j,i) = \mathrm{CFC}(j,i) - \mathrm{YD}(j,i). \tag{2.13}$$

Household disposable income, current consumption, and surplus and deficit are given by the sum of the corresponding values for the household's components:

$$\begin{cases} \mathrm{YD}(j) = \sum_i \mathrm{YD}(j,i) \\ \mathrm{CFC}(j) = \sum_i \mathrm{CFC}(j,i) \\ \mathrm{SUR}(j) = \sum_i \mathrm{SUR}(j,i) \\ \mathrm{DEF}(j) = \sum_i \mathrm{DEF}(j,i) \end{cases} \tag{2.14}$$

Household members with a deficit receive transfers (inflows) from household members with a surplus. If household disposable income is insufficient to fund current household private consumption, the household must fund the consumption of its deficit members by asset-based reallocations such as asset income or by dis-saving, if necessary. If household disposable income exceeds household consumption, the residual amount is assumed to be transferred to the head of household and saved.

The second step is to calculate a "tax rate" in order to estimate the proportion of individual surplus that must be transferred to fund the consumption of household members with a deficit. If the overall household deficit is higher than the household surplus, then the tax rate is equal to 1; otherwise the tax rate is given by the ratio between the household deficit and the household surplus:

$$\mathrm{tax}(j) = \min\left(1, \frac{\mathrm{DEF}(j)}{\mathrm{SUR}(j)}\right). \tag{2.15}$$

By assumption, any surplus held by members who are not the head of the household that is not taxed for current consumption transfers is assigned to the head of household to be saved. In other words, the head of household receives whatever surplus that is not transferred to other household members. The third step is to estimate intra-household transfer inflows and outflows, for which it is necessary to distinguish between the head of the household and its other members. For non-heads, intra-household transfer outflows are equal to the tax rate times the surplus; they equal zero for households with a deficit:

$$\mathrm{TFWO}(j,i) = \mathrm{tax}(j) \cdot \mathrm{SUR}(j,i). \tag{2.16}$$

For heads of households, the outflows consist of the tax rate times the surplus plus any shortfall that the head must fund using asset-based reallocations. For household members in deficit, intra-household transfer inflows are equal to their deficit, while for those in surplus they are equal to zero. For heads of households, transfer inflows are given by

$$\mathrm{TFWI}(i,j) = \mathrm{DEF}(i,j) + [\mathrm{DEF}(i) - \mathrm{SUR}(i)]. \tag{2.17}$$

In other words, if the household has an overall deficit, the head of household has to fund his or her own deficit through dis-saving or asset sales, which are not recorded as transfers but as asset-based reallocations (see Sect. 2.9.3). If the household has a surplus, the inflow is equal to the head of household's deficit plus the value of the surplus.

The fourth step is to estimate private intra-household transfers inflows and outflows by sector—education, health, other consumption—proportionally to the combined consumption of those household members with a deficit. Finally, per capita age profiles of intra-household transfer inflows and outflows are obtained as corresponding weighted age averages for all individuals in the sample. Net intra-household transfer is calculated as the difference between inflows and outflows.

2.9.3 Private Asset-Based Reallocations

Asset-based reallocations mediated by the private sector, like those mediated by the public sector, include two main flows: asset income and savings, representing an inflow and an outflow for individual household members, respectively (the SNA macro-aggregates of private asset income and savings are reported in Table 2.12 in the Appendix).

Private asset income consists of net property income plus capital income for households, corporations, and NPISH, whose aggregate values are provided by the SNA. Property income is classified by the NTA into two categories: interest and other property income. Private capital income (inclusive of taxes on production less subsides) is the return on capital owned by households and corporations and includes three components: (i) the net operating surplus of households, such as capital income arising from owner-occupied houses; (ii) the net operating surplus of corporations[9] and NPISH, measured as the difference between revenues and operating costs; and (iii) the portion of mixed income of the household sector that is

[9]The operating surplus of the corporate sector is included since it is not retained by the corporation but is distributed to the individuals who have provided the capital.

estimated to be a return to capital, assuming that one-third of mixed income is a return to capital and two-thirds is a return to labor.

As for most NTA countries (see Istenič et al. 2016), all asset income is by assumption assigned to the head of household, and age profiles of private asset-based reallocations are based on the age group of the head of household. However, age profiles of asset income have been estimated on the basis of microdata from the SHIW (Banca d'Italia 2008), which reports information on the distribution of asset income and savings by age and sex.

Finally, private savings are estimated as the final balancing item between age reallocations and the LCD or LCS at each age. By rearranging the terms used in the NTA budget, we obtain

$$S(x) = \mathrm{LCD}(x) - [\tau^{+}(x) - \tau^{-}(x)] - \mathrm{YA}(x). \tag{2.18}$$

In other words, savings are equal to the difference between net transfers plus asset income minus the LCD; if the former exceeds the latter, the difference is saved. Conversely, if the LCD exceeds net transfers and asset income, then consumption must be financed by dis-saving.

2.10 Smoothing and Macro-Control Adjustments

Per capita age profiles are mainly based on sample estimates. These estimates can be noisy due to sample errors, particularly at ages with relatively few observations like the oldest age groups. In order to reduce these kinds of variations, per capita age profiles are smoothed. However, in some cases significant age variations are not an effect of sample errors but reflect the actual age patterns of the phenomenon being considered. One example is the higher health consumption of newborns compared to the immediately subsequent ages. Another important example is represented by education consumption, especially in its public form, for which expenditures are significantly age-targeted and can be subject to significant changes from one year to another as a reflection of transitions to different levels of education. In such cases, the smoothing procedure has not been applied, since its purpose is to reduce only sampling variance, not actual variance.

Friedman's Super Smoother method (Friedman 1984) is used to smooth per capita age profiles through the supsum function in R software (http://www.r-project.org/), which incorporates sample weights. Once per capita age profiles are smoothed, preliminary aggregate age profiles can be estimated using population data by age; age averages are multiplied by the corresponding population size. Summing up preliminary estimates for all ages, we obtain an estimate of the total value for the overall population. However, this total may not coincide with the corresponding value provided by the SNA, so the estimates must be adjusted using a multiplicative factor given by the ratio between the SNA values and the estimated values developed in this chapter.

2.11 Concluding Remarks

This chapter has presented the specific data and methods used to estimate the economic lifecycle and age reallocations in Italy for 2008, based on the NTA methodological and conceptual framework. One of its aims was to make visible the linkage between the global NTA methodology as published by the United Nations (2013), the European harmonized methodology based on publicly available Eurostat data (Istenič et al. 2016), and the detailed NTA estimates at the national level, with Italy as a case study. While harmonized European data from the ESA have been used to derive the economic macro-aggregates, data at the national level have been used to derive age-specific averages of the economic macro-aggregates. In some cases original national files of microdata produced in the IESS framework on persons and households have been used. UDB IT-SILC microdata provided by Istat for the EU-SILC have been used to disaggregate labor income by single-year age groups. In other cases, specific data sources at the national level have been used; for example, SHIW data provided by Banca d'Italia have been employed to estimate age profiles of private asset income. Administrative data sources at the national level have also been used to derive age profiles of public consumption and transfers.

The chapter shows that in a number of cases the use of data sources available at the national level allowed for more detailed estimates of age-specific schedules of the economic activities. For example, the use of UDB IT-SILC microdata permitted detailed estimates even at older ages, whereas in the EU-SILC, the oldest elements of the population are aggregated into a single 80+ age group. UDB IT-SILC microdata also allowed for the direct calculation of age profiles of inter-household transfers, thus removing the simplifying head-of-household assumption and providing more accurate results. In fact, the use of specific data sources and specific methods can be implemented to obtain detailed estimates at the national level without significantly compromising opportunities for cross-country comparison. However, this would not be possible without the global NTA manual and the underlying research effort to standardize definitions and methodologies. The use of a European methodology built on harmonized Eurostat data sources represents a logical step for the systematic generation of the accounts for all European countries, which represents a highly desirable development for European statistics.

Appendix: Aggregate Macro-values

See Tables 2.3, 2.4, 2.5, 2.6, 2.7, 2.8, 2.9, 2.10, 2.11 and 2.12.

Table 2.3 Labor income, values at current prices, Italy 2008

Labor income and its components	Euro (million)	Percentage
Labor income	**830,248**	**100.0**
Earnings	680,279	81.9
Compensation of employees	*658,890*	*79.3*
Labor share of taxes less subsidies on production	*21,389*	*2.6*
Self-employment (labor share of gross mixed income)	149,969	18.1

Source Author's elaboration on Eurostat (2008a)

Table 2.4 Final consumption expenditure of households by purpose, values at current prices, Italy, 2008

Purpose of expenditure (COICOP Divisions)	Euro (million)	Percentage
Total	**978,916**	**100.0**
Food and nonalcoholic beverages	141,934	14.5
Alcoholic beverages, tobacco, and narcotics	40,546	4.1
Clothing and footwear	65,252	6.7
Housing, water, electricity, gas, and other fuels	210,522	21.5
Furnishings, household equipment, and routine maintenance	66,970	6.8
Health	31,197	3.2
Transport	125,003	12.8
Communications	26,735	2.7
Recreation and culture	67,023	6.9
Education	9170	0.9
Restaurants and hotels	89,232	9.1
Miscellaneous goods and services	105,333	10.8

Source Author's elaboration on Eurostat (2008b)

Table 2.5 General government: final consumption expenditure by function, values at current prices, Italy, 2008

Function of expenditure (COFOG divisions)	Euro (million)	Percentage
Total	**315,406**	**100.0**
General public services	41,707	13.2
Defense	22,093	7.0
Public order and safety	27,987	8.9
Economic affairs	22,284	7.1
Environment protection	4802	1.5
Housing and community amenities	6794	2.2
Health	108,363	34.4
Recreation, culture, and religion	6745	2.1
Education	60,661	19.2
Social protection	13,970	4.4

Source Author's elaboration on Eurostat (2008c)

Table 2.6 General government final consumptions expenditure for education groups, values at current prices, Italy, 2008

Code	Education COFOG groups	Euro (million)	%
09	**Education**	**60,661**	**100.0**
09.1	Pre-primary and primary education	22,412	37.0
09.2	Secondary education	30,439	50.2
09.3	Post-secondary non-tertiary education	791	1.3
09.4	Tertiary education	3283	5.4
09.5	Education not definable by level	702	1.2
09.6	Subsidiary services to education	2015	3.3
09.7	R&D Education	86	0.1
09.8	Education n.c.	933	1.5

Source Author's elaboration on Eurostat (2008c)

Table 2.7 General government final consumptions expenditure for health groups and classes, at current prices, Italy 2008

Code	Health COFOG groups and classes	Euro (million)	%
7	**Health**	**108,363**	**100.0**
7.1	Medical products, appliances, and equipment	12,287	11.3
7.1.1	*Pharmaceutical products*		
7.1.2	*Other medical products*		
7.1.3	*Therapeutic appliances and equipment*		
7.2	Outpatient services	32,933	30.4
7.2.1	*General medical services*		
7.2.2	*Specialized medical services*		
7.2.3	*Dental services*		
7.2.4	*Paramedical services*		
7.3	Hospital services	60,743	56.1
7.3.1	*General hospital services*		
7.3.2	*Specialized hospital services*		
7.3.3	*Medical and maternity center services*		
7.3.4	*Nursing and convalescent health services*		
7.4	Public health services	621	0.6
7.5	R&D health	899	0.8
7.6	Health n.e.c.	880	0.8

Source Author's elaboration on Eurostat (2008c)

Table 2.8 Hospital admissions and average cost by age and gender, Italy 2008

Age groups	Hospital admissions			Average cost		
	Male	Female	Total	Male	Female	Total
Total	**3,558,089**	**4,040,823**	**7,598,912**	**3511**	**3026**	**3253**
<1	150,144	122,156	272,300	2590	2586	2588
1–4	116,974	84,612	201,586	1771	1802	1784
5–9	77,249	55,523	132,772	1802	1867	1829
10–14	70,494	51,862	122,356	1957	1983	1968
15–19	83,896	80,740	164,636	2374	2038	2209
20–24	86,823	146,217	233,040	2533	1983	2188
25–29	92,171	253,028	345,199	2623	1965	2141
30–34	112,375	363,529	475,904	2723	1987	2161
35–39	133,124	309,961	443,085	2869	2139	2358
40–44	156,090	204,747	360,837	3084	2544	2778
45–49	168,773	177,369	346,142	3326	2861	3088
50–54	190,276	179,154	369,430	3584	3048	3324
55–59	237,444	194,627	432,071	3823	3324	3598
60–64	293,139	223,320	516,459	3992	3550	3801
65–69	355,054	268,883	623,937	4105	3770	3961
70–74	384,834	312,043	696,877	4171	3957	4075
75+	849,229	1,013,052	1,862,281	4009	3900	3950

Source Ministero della Salute (2008)

Table 2.9 Public transfers inflows classified by NTA Sectors, Italy, 2008

NTA Sectors	Values at current prices (euro, million)			Percentage values		
	In-kind	Cash	Total	In-kind	Cash	Total
All sectors	**315,406**	**287,450**	**602,856**	**100.0**	**100.0**	**100.0**
Education	60,661	0	60,661	19.2	0.0	10.1
Health care	108,363	8076	116,406	34.3	2.8	19.3
Social protection	13,970	267,420	281,390	4.4	93.0	46.7
Old age	*5395*	*193,249*	*198,644*	*1.7*	*67.2*	*33.0*
Other Social Protection	*8575*	*74,171*	*82,746*	*2.7*	*25.8*	*13.7*
Other public transfers	132,445	11,954	144,399	42.0	4.2	23.9

Source Author's elaboration on Eurostat (2008c, d)

Table 2.10 Other Social Protection classified by functions, values at current prices, Italy, 2008

Functions	Euro (million)	Percentage
Other Social Protection	**82,746**	**100.0**
Disability	22,700	27.4
Survivors	36,636	44.3
Family and Children	15,144	18.3
Unemployment	7508	9.1
Housing	0	0.0
Social exclusion n.e.c.	758	0.9

Source Author's elaboration on Eurostat (2008d)

Table 2.11 Public asset-based reallocations, at current prices, Italy 2008

Public asset-based reallocations	Euro (million)
Net Public Transfers	**0**
Public Transfer Inflows	602,856
In-kind	*309,512*
Cash	*293,344*
Public Transfer Outflows	602,856
Taxes and Social contributions	*649,086*
Transfer Surplus/Deficit	*−46,230*
Public Asset-based Reallocation	−46,230
Public Asset Income	*−62,246*
Public Saving	*−16,015*

Source Author's elaborations on Eurostat (2008a)

Table 2.12 Private asset-based reallocations, at current prices, Italy 2008

Private asset-based reallocations	Euro (million)
Private asset-based reallocations	**320,886**
Private asset income	**377,910**
Private capital income	324,727
Private property income, net	53,183
Private interest, net	*49,248*
Private other property income, net	*3935*
Private saving	**57,024**

Source Author's elaborations on Eurostat (2008a)

References

Agenzia Italiana del Farmaco, Gruppo di lavoro OsMed. (2010). *L'uso dei farmaci in Italia. Rapporto nazionale anno 2009.* Roma: Il Pensiero Scientifico Editore.

Deming, W. E., & Stephan, F. F. (1940). On a least squares adjustment of a sampled frequency table when the expected marginal totals are known. *The Annals of Mathematical Statistics, 11* (4), 427–444.

Eurostat. (2008e). *The European system of integrated social protection statistics (ESSPROS) Manual.* Luxembourg: Office for Official Publication of the European Communities.

Eurostat. (2011). *Manual on sources and methods for the compilation of COFOG Statistics*. Luxembourg: Publication Office of the European Union. http://ec.europa.eu/eurostat/documents/3859598/5917333/KS-RA-11-013-EN.PDF/2eb9714a-ee4b-49fe-baab-e9af5ca457b1. Accessed December 4, 2016.
Eurostat. (2013). *European system of accounts—ESA 2010*. Luxembourg: Publications Office of the European Union. http://ec.europa.eu/eurostat/documents/3859598/5925693/KS-02-13-269-EN.PDF/44cd9d01-bc64-40e5-bd40-d17df0c69334. Accessed December 4, 2016.
Friedman, J. H. (1984). SMART User's Guide. *Technical Report* (1), Department of Statistics, Stanford University.
Istenič, T., Šeme, A., Hammer, B., Lotrič Dolinar, A., & Sambt, J. (2016). *The European NTA Manual*. New York: United Nations. http://ntaccounts.org/doc/repository/NTA%20manual%202013.pdf. Accessed December 4, 2016.
Lee, R. (1994a). The formal demography of population aging, transfers, and the economic life cycle. In L. G. Martin & S. H. Preston (Eds.), *Demography of aging* (pp. 8–49). Washington, DC: National Academies Press.
Lee, R. (1994b). Population age structure, intergenerational transfer, and wealth: A new approach, with applications to the United States. *Journal of Human Resources, 29*(4), 1027–1063.
Lee, R., & Mason, A. (2011). *Population aging and the generational economy: A global perspective*. Northampton, MA.: Edward Elgar Publishing.
Mason, A., Lee, R., Donehower, G., Lee, S., Miller, T., Tung, A. C., et al. (2009). National Transfer Accounts manual: Draft version 1.0. NTA Working Papers (WP 08-09).
Ministero della Salute. (2008). *Rapporto annuale sull'attività di ricovero ospedaliero. Dati SDO 2008*. http://www.salute.gov.it/imgs/c_17_pubblicazioni_1253_allegato.pdf. Accessed December 28, 2016.
Ministero dell' Economia e della Finanza. (2009). *Le tendenze di medio-lungo periodo del sistema pensionistico e socio-sanitario 2009*. Rapporto n. 11 anno 2009. http://www.rgs.mef.gov.it/_Documenti/VERSIONE-I/Attivit–i/Spesa-soci/Attivita_di_previsione_RGS/2010/Le-tendenze-di-m-l-periodo-del-sistema-pensionistico-e-socio-sanitario—Rapporto-n11.pdf. Accessed December 28, 2016.
Samuelson, P. A. (1958) An Exact Consumption-Loan Model of Interest with or without the Social Contrivance of Money. J*ournal of Political Economy*, *66*(6), 467–482.
United Nations. (2000). *Classification of expenditure according to purpose*. New York: United Nations. http://unstats.un.org/unsd/EconStatKB/Attachment222.aspx?AttachmentType=1. Accessed December 4, 2016.
United Nations. (2013). *National transfer accounts manual: Measuring and analysing the generational economy*. New York: United Nations. http://www.un.org/en/development/desa/population/publications/pdf/development/NTA_Manual_12June2013.pdf. Accessed December 4, 2016.

Statistical Sources

Banca d'Italia. (2008). Indagine sui bilanci delle famiglie italiane.
Eurostat. (2008a). Annual sector accounts. http://ec.europa.eu/eurostat/web/sector-accounts/data/database. Accessed December 28, 2016.
Eurostat. (2008b). Government finance statistics, annual government statistics, final consumption expenditure of households by consumption purpose (COICOP). https://data.europa.eu/euodp/it/data/dataset/E3td1eJcpRfbHOtLntXwA. Accessed December 28, 2016.

Eurostat. (2008c). Government finance statistics, annual government statistics, general government expenditure by function (COFOG). http://appsso.eurostat.ec.europa.eu/nui/show.do?dataset=gov_a_exp&lang=en. Accessed December 28, 2016.

Eurostat. (2008d). European system of integrated social protection statistics (ESSPROS). http://ec.europa.eu/eurostat/statistics-explained/index.php/Social_protection_statistics. Accessed December 28, 2016.

Eurostat. (2010). Statistics, population data. http://ec.europa.eu/eurostat/web/population-demography-migration-projections/population-data/database. Accessed December 28, 2016.

Istat. (2008a). Indagine sui consumi delle famiglie.

Istat. (2008b). Multiscopo sulle famiglie: condizioni di salute e ricorso ai servizi sanitari.

Istat. (2008c). Multiscopo sulle famiglie: uso del tempo.

Istat. (2009). Indagine sulle condizioni di vita.

Chapter 3
Age, Economy, and Welfare

Abstract This chapter presents the main results for the economic lifecycle and intergenerational reallocation system related to Italy in 2008, based on the NTA conceptual and methodological framework. Specific attention is paid to the role of families and the state in financing the consumption of dependent ages. Results show that the actual age borders of economic dependence vary considerably from those conventionally used in demography. The detailed analysis of public transfers shows the prevalence of redistribution addressed to old age protection and a lack of resources toward the specific social needs and risks of prime-age adults. Results for the household institutional sector show the key role of families in sustaining the prolonged dependence of adult children.

3.1 Introduction

Statistical information in virtually all fields of social concern has improved significantly over the last hundred years. Ameliorations in national accounting have been particularly evident in the years since the Great Depression. However, it was only after the experience of the Second World War that the need for international accounting standards was stressed and that the SNA was first published (United Nations 1953). As a part of the 1993 SNA revision (United Nations 1993), the scope of national accounting has been broadened to reflect the increasing complexity of societies through the development of satellite accounts for a number of aspects in relevant fields (e.g., social protection and environmental protection expenditures). Behind the impressive advancements in the development and use of SNA data, changes in social concerns over recent decades require new adjustments in the architecture of national accounts (Vanioli 2014). The looming presence of aging societies now calls for further advancements in statistical information, especially for the development of social welfare and age-related economic measures in public accounting.

The debate around measures of social welfare arose as soon as the first national accounts were created (Kuznets 1934) and has recently been rekindled by the

M. Zannella, *The Economic Lifecycle, Gender and Intergenerational Support*, SpringerBriefs in Population Studies, DOI 10.1007/978-3-319-62669-7_3

Stiglitz Report (Stiglitz et al. 2009). Efforts to analyze the generational dimension of the economy date back to Samuelson's (1958) overlapping generations model. The 1990s witnessed a renewed interest in the state's redistributive function across generations, with studies focusing largely on fiscal sustainability and equity (e.g., Auerbach et al. 1994) and on the longstanding dispute on the intergenerational conflict (Preston 1984) or contract (Bengtson and Achenbaum 1993; Walker 1996). However, debates on intergenerational issues have focused almost entirely on the public sector, and it has been only recently that financial support within the family has begun to capture the attention of scholars (e.g., Albertini et al. 2007).

A lack of data has led to partial or fragmentary analysis of aging and the generational questions around families or the state, whereas a complete understanding of the generational economy requires a systematic analysis of both the private and public institutional sectors and of their interaction. In recent years, the NTA has developed an international standard to set up age-specific national accounts and measure intergenerational exchange in the economy comprehensively (see Lee and Mason 2011). The NTA is designed to complement SNA by developing satellite accounts for age-specific economic activities (United Nations 2013).

In this chapter, the main results based on the NTA for Italy in 2008 are presented. An extensive database has been developed, containing age profiles of production, consumption, transfer payments, and benefits for both the public and private sectors. The age profiles can be estimated in both per capita and aggregate terms. Per capita age profiles (measured in euros) express the annual amount of SNA quantities for an average individual at a given age. Aggregate age profiles (measured in millions of euros) are calculated as the product between per capita age profiles of the economic quantities and the corresponding population size and thus reflect both the age-specific schedules of economic activities and the demographic structure of the population. The following age profiles are shown and discussed in this chapter: labor income, public and private consumption, public and private transfer inflows (by function) and outflows, and public and private savings and asset income. The private sector refers to households and NPISH, although the vast majority of private transfers are household transfers. Full results encompass estimates of age profiles for more than 90 economic variables.

The chapter is structured as follows. Section 3.2 presents the main results for age profiles of private and public consumption, with spending further disaggregated according to purpose (education, health, and other consumption) in sect. 3.2.1. Section 3.3 shows the age profiles of labor income and its components, earnings and self-employment. The economic lifecycle along with its elements are presented and discussed in Sect. 3.4. Sections 3.5 and 3.6 respectively present the public and private intergenerational reallocation systems; Sect. 3.5.1 offers an overview of public transfer inflows detailed by function. Finally, Sect. 3.7 provides a comprehensive picture of the economic lifecycle and the intergenerational reallocation system for Italy in 2008. Intergenerational reallocations as a source for financing consumption are discussed, with particular regard to families' role in sustaining children and young adults. Section 3.8 concludes.

3.2 Consumption

Figure 3.1 shows annual per capita age profiles of consumption and its two broad components of public and private consumption, which behave differently with age; the former prevails at young ages from 0 to 14 years, while the latter dominates middle and older ages. Public consumption peaks at age 0, when public spending for newborns reaches the value of €6000 per year and then falls rapidly. It starts to increase again around the age of three and forms a slope through age 14, when it shows a sharp decline. It remains almost constant during the prime-age years and rises gradually after age 60. Private consumption increases with age, staying almost constant during adult ages, with two exceptions at childbearing and retirement ages, and a moderate downturn at older ages.

At the aggregate level, public and private consumption make up 28.9 and 71.1% of total consumption, respectively. However, looking at the detailed categories of expenditure makes it possible to observe that public spending is the main source of financing for education and health consumption. More precisely, public consumption is made up of 19.2% for education, 34.4% for health, and 46.4% for other public goods (Table 2.5, Chap. 2). On the other hand, education and health constitute only 4.1% of private consumption, with the remaining 95.9% being expenditures for current consumption and durables (Table 2.4, Chap. 2). In the next subsections, detailed age profiles of private and public consumption by purpose of expenditure are analyzed to improve our understanding of age-specific needs and the role of families and the state in providing for those needs.

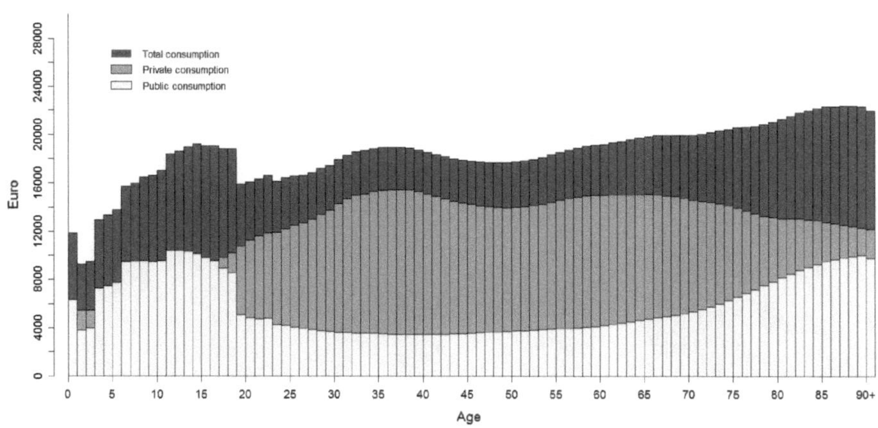

Fig. 3.1 Per capita age profiles of consumption. *Source* Author's elaborations on Eurostat (2008b, c), Istat (2008a) and various other sources

3.2.1 Consumption by Institutional Sector and Expenditure

We must start with an initial insight on the role of households and the state in financing individuals' consumption. In particular, private and public consumption expenditure by age for education, health, and other consumption are compared in order to highlight the contribution of the private and public sectors in addressing social needs during the different stages of the life course. Figure 3.2 shows the age profiles of public and private consumption for education.

Public expenditures make up the great majority of expenditures for education. Public consumption for education begins at kindergarten ages—such expenditures on education for younger children are negligible—and is characterized by a stepped pattern that reflects changes in public spending related to transitions across different levels of education. Public consumption for education peaks at age 12, when the average expenditure for pupils reaches the value of €7000 per year and then declines rapidly, especially after age 14 when compulsory schooling ends. Public spending on education shows another small peak for adults aged 19–22 years, after which it decreases monotonically with age. Private expenditure for education is, on average, much lower compared to public expenditure until age 20, when households and the state begin to spend similar amounts of money, highlighting the fundamental role of families in financing tertiary education. Private consumption for education has its highest per capita values between ages 19 and 26 and then declines. Both public and private spending for education virtually disappear before age 30.

Public and private health consumption show a peak at age 0 due to birth-related costs, even though the peak has much higher values for public than for private spending (Fig. 3.3). After that, public consumption decreases rapidly and remains almost constant until age 40, when it starts to increase gradually. From age 60

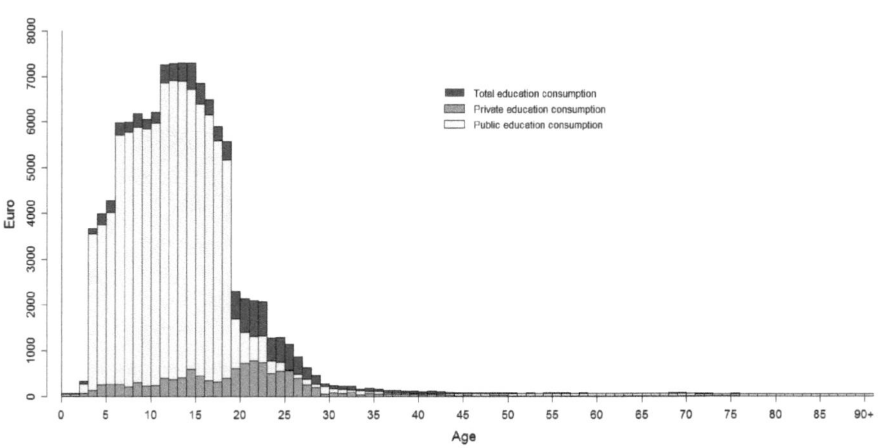

Fig. 3.2 Per capita age profiles of education consumption. *Source* Author's elaborations on Eurostat (2008b, c), Istat (2008a) and various other sources

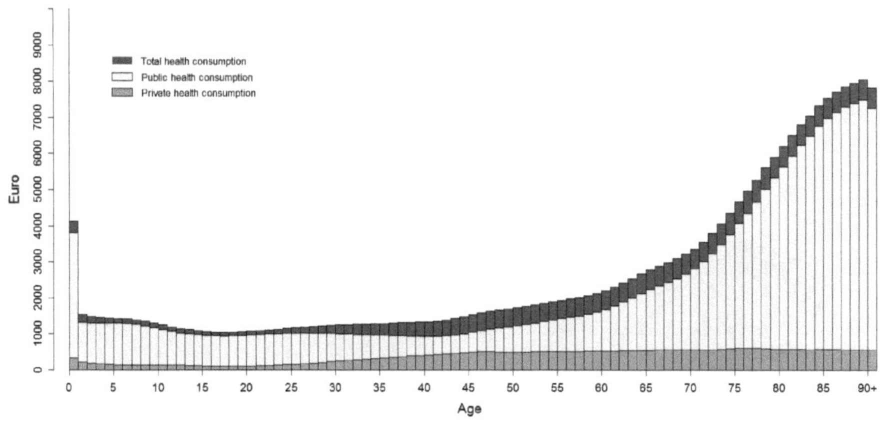

Fig. 3.3 Per capita age profiles of health consumption. *Source* Author's elaborations on Eurostat (2008b, c), Istat (2008a, b) and various other sources

onward, the pace of the increase becomes considerably more rapid due to the deterioration in health conditions at older ages and greater related costs. Private consumption is low during younger ages, starts to increase slightly after age 30, and then remains almost constant during adult ages with no significant increase at older ages, strikingly different from what is observed in the public sector.

Table 3.1 reports the per capita values and the relative distribution of public health consumption by broad age groups and expenditure subcategories. As discussed in Chap. 2, hospital services represent the main public expenditure in Italy

Table 3.1 Public health consumption by COFOG function and age group, Italy, 2008

	All	0	1–14	15–59	60–69	70–79	80+
Per capita (euro)							
Total	**1810**	**3828**	**1124**	**1082**	**2133**	**3876**	**7016**
Medical products	205	144	116	156	309	419	459
Outpatience services	550	735	718	500	500	592	701
Hospital services	1015	2909	250	385	1284	2825	5816
Other Public health services	40	40	40	40	40	40	40
Percentage composition by COFOG group							
Total	**100.0**	**100.0**	**100.0**	**100.0**	**100.0**	**100.0**	**100.0**
Medical products	11.3	3.8	10.3	14.5	14.5	10.8	6.5
Outpatience services	30.4	19.2	63.9	46.2	23.4	15.3	10.0
Hospital services	56.1	76.0	22.2	35.6	60.2	72.9	82.9
Other Public health services	2.2	1.0	3.6	3.7	1.9	1.0	0.6

Source Own elaborations on Eurostat (2008c), Istat (2008b) and various other sources

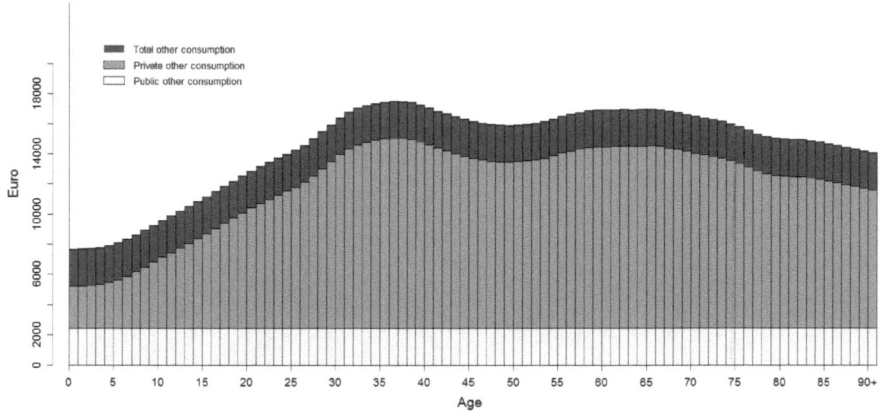

Fig. 3.4 Per capita age profiles of other consumption. *Source* Author's elaborations on Eurostat (2008b, c), Istat (2008a) and various other sources

(Table 2.7, Chap. 2). The highest per capita values of health expenditure are found in the age group of those 80 and older (an average of €7016 per year), with hospital services representing 82.9% of heath expenditure for this age group. These findings appear to support pessimistic interpretations of population aging, according to which aging societies will face increasing health costs for the state that will squeeze resources out of the taxpayers. However, we know from more optimistic views that a number of factors, including behavioral changes like healthier lifestyles and a compression of morbidity, may attenuate the impact of population aging on public finances (e.g., Bloom et al. 2010). Human capital theory has shown that improvements in education contribute greatly to developing the resources needed to achieve better health (e.g., Mushkin 1962).

Figure 3.4 reports per capita age profiles of total, public, and private consumption other than education and health. Other public consumption refers to collective goods and services (defense, justice, environmental protection, etc.) that are assigned in equal shares to all members of the population, giving rise to a flat age profile. Per capita age profiles of other private consumption grow rapidly until approximately age 30 and then remain almost constant during middle ages before decreasing slightly beginning at around age 70. Private consumption other than education and health shows two bulges around ages 30–40 and ages 60–70, reflecting the life course stages of family formation and retirement ages, during which individuals are likely to spend more money on items like durable goods.

In summary, differences in age patterns of public and private consumption are due mainly to the existence of universal education and health programs in Italy, on the one hand, and to high levels of private consumption during adulthood explained by the predominance of other consumption, on the other hand.

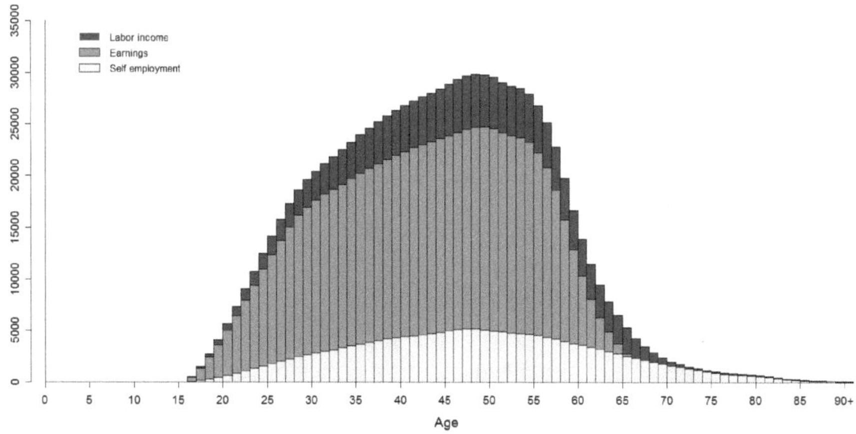

Fig. 3.5 Per capita age profiles of labor income. *Source* Author's elaborations on Eurostat (2008a) and Istat (2009)

3.3 Labor Income

Labor income is composed of 81.9% in wage earnings and 18.1% in self-employment. Self-employment is relatively high in Italy, where Eurostat data indicate it represented 26% of total employment in 2008, about 11% higher than the European average (http://ec.europa.eu/eurostat/data/browse-statistics-by-theme). This is due mainly to the role of small- and medium-sized enterprises in the Italian economy, especially in manufacturing. Per capita age profiles of wage earnings and self-employment highlight these differences in both shape and levels (Fig. 3.5). As for the shape, the main differences involve the average ages of entry into and exit from the labor market. Wage earnings begin at age 15,[1] whereas self-employments starts slightly later, though both reach a peak around age 48. Then, labor income starts to decline from age 58 until it almost disappears at age 70, whereas, self-employment lasts more than 10 years longer. Self-employment may also represent a strategy for employees to continue working and earning money after retiring from wage-paying employment. Self-employment shows considerably lower levels than wage earnings due to the corresponding lower participation rates for this activity. However, the relatively low values may be partly due also to the under-reporting of this kind of income.

Finally, it should be noted that as a result of the reform of the pension system, criteria to access pensions (age or years of contribution) have undergone changes in

[1]Information on labor income is only reported in the EU-SILC from age 15 onward, reflecting the Italian law on the minimum age for access to the labor market.

Italy. Starting in January 2012, age at retirement has been raised to 66 years[2] for those with at least 20 years of pension contributions, alternatively the requirement is about 42 years of contributions. Furthermore, disincentives for early retirement and incentives for delayed retirement have been introduced. This will probably be reflected in the shape and levels of earnings in the future, shifting the tail of the labor income curve toward older ages.

3.4 The Economic Lifecycle

The economic lifecycle is described by the age patterns of consumption and production. The LCD or LCS is obtained as the difference between consumption and labor income at each age. In particular, a positive value in this difference means that consumption is greater than labor income, giving rise to an LCD. Conversely, a negative value indicates an excess of labor income over consumption, generating an LCS. As discussed in Chap. 1, the LCD or LCS can be used as the basis for calculating indicators of the effective economic dependence in a country; while traditional demographic indicators of economic dependence are based on exogenously fixed age limits (e.g., 0–14 years qualifies as "young" or age 65 and above is defined as "old"), the NTA age boundaries of the economic activity or dependence of a population are endogenously determined by age profiles of consumption and labor income.

Figure 3.6 displays per capita age profiles of the economic lifecycle and its two components: combined public and private consumption and labor income. As expected, two age groups experience an LCD (meaning that they depend on age reallocation to finance their own consumption): the young and those who are 59 and older, for whom the term "mature" will be used. The word "mature" in this context is chosen because "old" and especially "elderly" are neither suitable to nor always appreciated by those who are just past this threshold and because "elderly" will likely convey the notion of frailty to most readers. The actual age borders of economic dependence and activity differ significantly from the traditional choices. Children are economically dependent from age 0 to age 26, with an LCD peak at age 14, when its value reaches €20,062 per year on average. The LCD then becomes an LCS at age 27 until age 58. LCDs return at age 59, when the consumption curve again overtakes the labor income curve, rising to over €20,000 per year for ages 80 and above. Thus, the LCS lasted for 30 years in Italy, using 2008 numbers. Conventional age borders of economic dependency not only ignore the actual age patterns of consumption and labor income but also the related heterogeneity across countries. Hammer et al. (2015) analyzed economic dependence for a number of European countries in 2011. The study reports that crossover ages from

[2]A gradual shift in the age at retirement was legislated for women; they must extend their working lives to age 62 by 2012 and to age 66 by 2018.

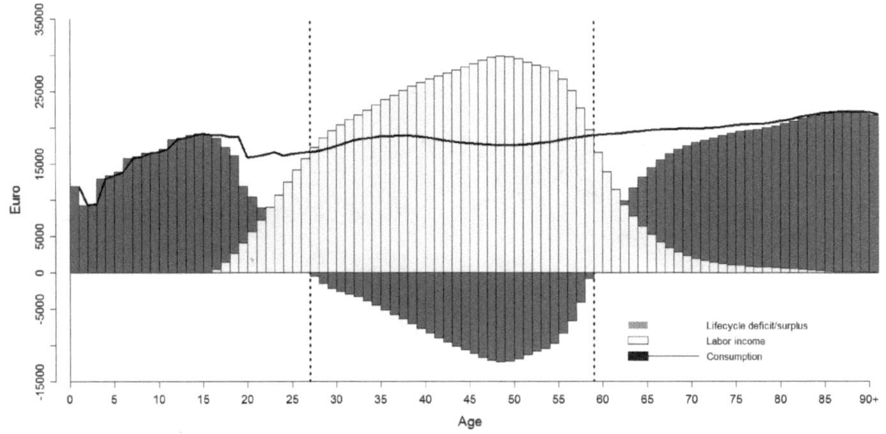

Fig. 3.6 Per capita age profiles of lifecycle deficit. *Source* Author's elaborations on Eurostat (2008a, b, c), Istat (2008a, 2009) and various other sources

LCD to LCS varied between age 24 (Austria) and 27 (Italy) for the young and between age 58 (Slovenia) and 64 (Sweden) for the mature. The differences can become even larger in comparison with lower income economies, as Mejía-Guevara (2011) showed for Mexico, where the NTA-based economic dependence of the young runs from age 0 to 33 and that of the mature cohort starts at age 48, with an average LCS duration of only 14 years (from ages 34–47).

The main differences between per capita and aggregate economic lifecycle (the latter is shown in Fig. 3.7) appear in consumption at adult and mature ages. The per capita age profile of consumption remains constant from age 20 until a slight increase at mature ages, whereas aggregate profiles show a bulge in the middle years and then a decrease at mature ages, reflecting the age distribution of the overall population. In aggregate terms, the value of the LCD for both the young and the mature amounts to €464,019 million, while the LCS is equal to €204,498 million. The value of the total net deficit[3] for the Italian population in 2008 is thus €259,521 million. As regards deficit ages, the young and the mature make up 43.3 and 56.7% of the overall LCD, respectively, at €201,042 million and €262,977 million.

Italy is among European countries with the highest levels of economic dependence measured by LCD among both the young and the mature, raising concerns about the sustainability of consumption in the long run (see Hammer et al. 2015). Table 3.2 shows a simulation of the future evolution of the economic lifecycle that reports aggregate LCD and LCS for deficit and surplus ages, respectively, at three points in time: 2008, 2020, and 2050. The values have been estimated using UN population projections (United Nations 2011), behind the simplifying assumption

[3]Net deficit refers to the total value of the LCD of the young and the mature net of the value of the LCS generated by the working age population.

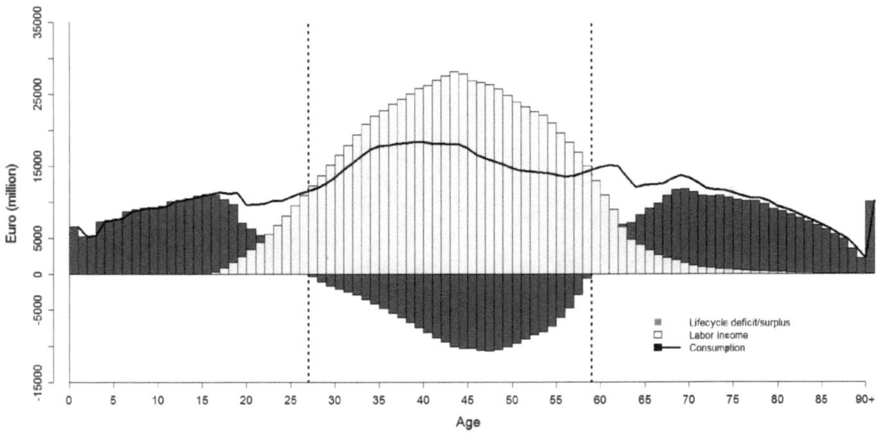

Fig. 3.7 Aggregate age profiles of lifecycle deficit. *Source* Author's elaborations on Eurostat (2008a, b, c), Istat (2008a, 2009) and various other sources

Table 3.2 Aggregate values of the LCD and LCS in 2008, 2020 and 2050

Aggregate values (millions of euro)			
	2008	2020	2050
Total LCD	464,019	505,393	601,985
LCD young ages	*201,042*	*200,623*	*188,583*
LCD mature ages	*262,977*	*304,770*	*413,402*
LCS ages	204,498	215,678	179,485
Deficit net of surplus	259,521	289,715	422,500
Relative variation (%)			
	2008–2020	2020–2050	2008–2050
Total LCD	8.9	19.1	29.7
LCD young ages	*−0.2*	*−6.0*	*−6.2*
LCD mature ages	*15.9*	*35.6*	*57.2*
LCS ages	5.5	−16.8	−12.2
Deficit net of surplus	11.6	45.8	62.8
Annual relative variation (%)			
	2008–2020	2020–2050	2008–2050
Total LCD	0.7	0.6	0.7
LCD young ages	*0.0*	*−0.2*	*−0.1*
LCD mature ages	*1.3*	*1.2*	*1.4*
LCS ages	0.5	−0.6	−0.3
Deficit net of surplus	1.0	1.5	1.5

Source Author's elaborations from United Nations (2011) and various other sources

of constant per capita age profiles of labor income and consumption. As a pure effect of change in population age structure, the total deficit net of the surplus for the population would increase by 11.6% by 2020 and by 62.8% by 2050. Thus, the average annual increase is 1.5% for the entire span of time (2008–2050), 1.0% from 2008 to 2020, and 1.5% from 2020 to 2050. The increase in the net deficit is caused by two main interacting factors: an LCS decrease due to a shrinking working age population and an increase in LCD among the mature by 57.2% from 2008 to 2050. Conversely, the share of the LCD among the young would decrease by 6.2% during the whole period as a consequence of the declining proportion of the population at younger ages.

3.5 The Public Intergenerational Reallocation System

The public inter-age reallocation system refers to flows of current resources mediated by government and regulated by two main economic mechanisms: transfers and asset-based reallocations. Public transfers consist of flows with different directions: inflows from the state to the beneficiaries of public programs and outflows from taxpayers to the state, the proceeds of which are used to finance public programs (Fig. 3.8). At young ages, inflows are mostly provided in the form of in-kind services and hence reflect the shape of per capita age profiles in public consumption, with a peak at age 0 due to birth-related health costs and a stepped pattern at school ages due to education expenditures. Prime-age adults (aged approximately 20–50) are those receiving the smallest amount of resources from the state, highlighting a rather flat age profile of public transfer inflows. Starting at around age 55, the per capita age profiles of public transfers received increase rapidly, peaking at the very oldest ages. Public transfer outflows show a similar reverse-U shape to labor income but with broader age borders; they start at very young ages due to the value-added taxes (VAT)[4] on consumption and remain through mature ages, due mainly to taxes on revenues and assets. Net public transfers are positive for children until age 20, meaning that they are net beneficiaries of public programs; then they become negative until age 60, when people are net givers within the state, and, finally, turn positive again at mature ages.

At the aggregate level, net transfers are equal to zero when public inflows and outflows are perfectly balanced. However, this situation is unlikely. Inflows to the beneficiaries of public programs can exceed outflows from taxpayers, generating a transfer deficit, or, as in the case of Italy,[5] there can be an excess of outflows on inflows, generating a surplus. As discussed in Chap. 2, public asset-based

[4]VAT is assigned to age according to private consumption age profiles.

[5]The mechanism underlying the public reallocation system is shown in Table 2.11 in Chap. 2, reporting aggregate values for public transfer inflows, public transfer outflows, public transfer deficit/surplus, public asset-based reallocation, public asset income, and public savings.

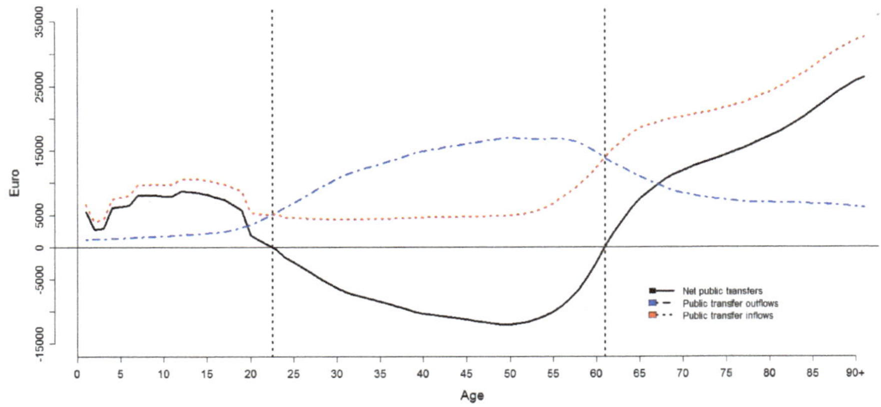

Fig. 3.8 Per capita age profiles of public transfers. *Source* Author's elaborations on Eurostat (2008a, c, d), Istat (2009) and various other sources

reallocations (i.e. asset income less savings) are the balancing item between public transfer outflows and inflows; at the aggregate level, they must equal the transfer deficit or surplus. The mismatch between transfer inflows and outflows can be financed with public asset income or dis-saving in the case of a transfer deficit and thus represent an inflow for residents. Public asset-based reallocations are negative in the case of a transfer surplus (Fig. 3.9); the excess of outflows from taxpayers on transfer inflows is used by the government for savings and asset income such as paying interest on public debt, thus representing an outflow for residents. It should be recalled that the age profiles of public asset-based reallocations and their components reflect the age schedule of taxpayers; indeed, they reach their higher levels during the working years.

3.5.1 Public Transfer Inflows by Function

Public transfer inflows include a number of expenditures that display significantly different behavior with age (Fig. 3.10). Specifically, public transfer inflows are composed by social expenditures for education, health, pensions, and social protection other than pensions in cash and in kind. It should be recalled that in-kind inflows are equal to public consumption. Pensions are considered separately from other cash inflows because of both their intrinsic age distribution and their sheer magnitude.

Education and health make up 10.1 and 19.3% of total inflows, respectively (Table 2.9, Chap. 2). While education inflows are concentrated at younger ages and virtually disappear at age 30, inflows for health show increasing per capita values with age. Other public transfers represent 24.0% of the total inflows and consist of collective services that by definition are distributed equally among all members of

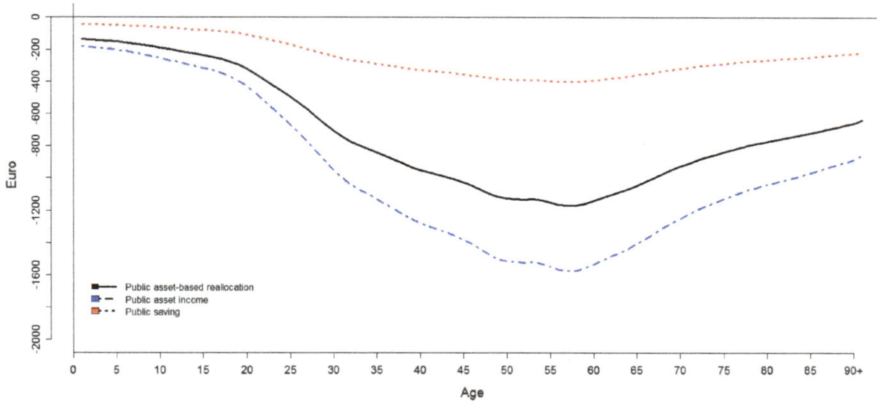

Fig. 3.9 Per capita age profiles of public asset-based reallocation. *Source* Author's elaborations on Eurostat (2008a), Istat (2009), Banca d'Italia (2008)

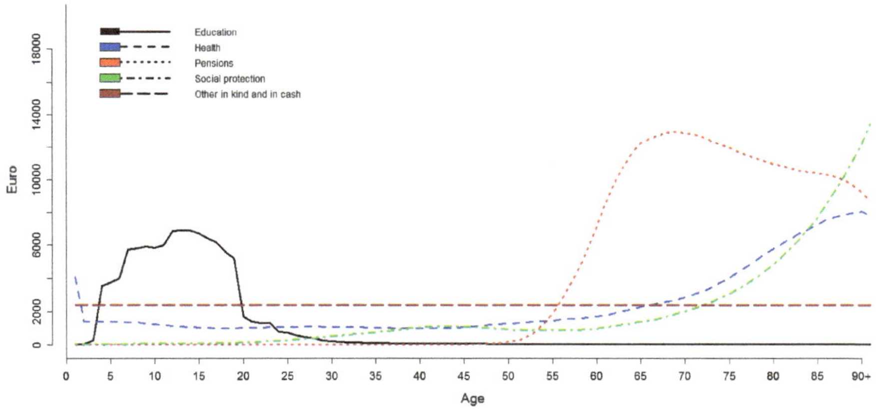

Fig. 3.10 Per capita age profiles of public transfer inflows. *Source* Author's elaborations on Eurostat (2008a, c, d) and various other sources

the population. Public pensions constitute 33.0% of total public transfer inflows and peak at age 68, when an average individual receives around €13,000 annually in pension. Social protection other than pensions (13.7% of total inflows) is flat at young ages, starts to rise gradually at age 20 through age 50, and then increases rapidly at mature ages.

Social protection other than pensions is composed of expenditures for survivors (44.3%), disability (27.4%), families and children (18.3%), unemployment (9.1%), and miscellaneous (0.9%). Other social protection is negligible through age 20. It shows a small bulge in the middle years mostly attributable to public spending for families and children. However, individuals in the middle years of life receive on average less than €1000 per year from the government for social protection, including unemployment and family allowances. Public spending for social

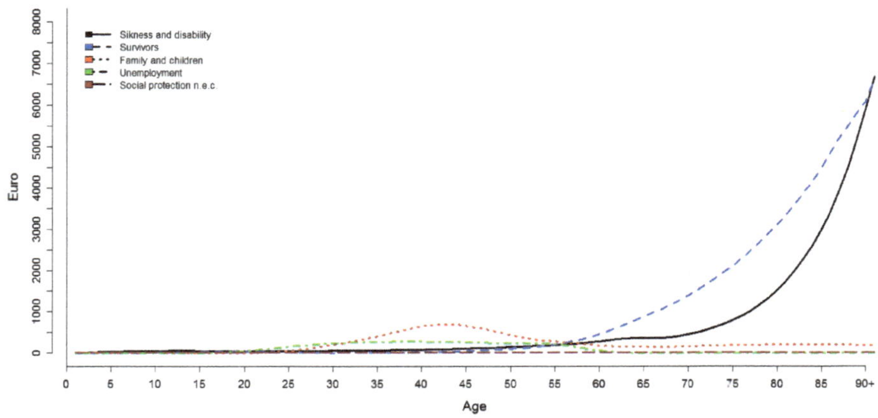

Fig. 3.11 Per capita age profile of social protection other than pensions. *Source* Author's elaborations on Eurostat (2008a, c, d) and various other sources

protection other than pensions starts to increase rapidly from age 60 onward due to expenditures for survivors and disability and is more than €10,000 per year for the average individual at the oldest ages.

Figure 3.11 presents the detailed categories of expenditure of social protection (other than pensions) by broad age groups. The highest share of total other social protection is concentrated at mature ages (61.9%) due to expenditures for disability and survivors (equal to 77.5 and 85.5% of the total in-kind expenditure for this age group), followed by ages 30–49 with a share of 20.9% of overall inflows, explained mostly by expenditures for families and children and unemployment (64.6 and 65.9% of the expenditure for this age group).

As discussed in Chap. 1, the main purpose of welfare systems is to protect members of society from risks and addressing their needs through a redistributive function. Public redistribution can be divided into three main categories: horizontal, vertical, and intergroup (Hills 2004; Esping-Andersen et al. 2009). Horizontal redistribution seeks to reallocate resources across the lifecycle and is represented well by Barr's analogy of the welfare state as a collective "piggy bank" (Barr 2001). Pensions are one example. The vertical dimension is meant to ensure equality across different income groups; borrowing an expression from Esping-Andersen et al. (2009), vertical distribution represents the "Robin Hood role"; resources are shifted from the richer to the poorer largely through the progressivity of the tax system and through social assistance programs. Finally, redistribution between groups consists of redistribution to groups with specific needs, such as allowances and other benefits to families with children. The results of the detailed analysis of public inflows for Italy in 2008 reveal two main highlights: the prevalence of horizontal redistribution addressed to old age protection and the scarcity of vertical and intergroup redistribution, particularly with regard to effective social protection targeted to the specific needs of prime-age adults (e.g., housing, unemployment, family allowances, etc.). This arrangement can be considered doubly biased, since not only are the needs of young adults and middle-aged people largely ignored, but the fiscal burden is also mainly sustained through their efforts.

3.6 The Private Intergenerational Reallocation System

Like the public sector, private reallocation can occur in the form of direct transfers and asset-based reallocations; the latter are determined by patterns of asset income and savings by age. It should be recalled that private savings are considered as the final balancing item in the NTA and consist of the intergenerational flows necessary to fund that part of consumption that is not already financed through labor income or age reallocations. Figure 3.12 presents per capita age profiles of net private transfers and its components: inflows and outflows. Private transfers can occur within the same household (intra-household) or between different households (inter-household). Given that intra-household transfers represent the great majority of private transfers (97%), the text below refers to intra-household transfers as private transfers. Children from age 0 to age 18 are pure beneficiaries of private transfers, since they receive inflows while they do not make any transfers to other age groups. On average, children start to pay private transfers at age 19. However, they become net givers only from age 29, when the amount of resources transferred begins to exceed that of resources received. Private transfer outflows are very important during the adult working ages, peaking at age 47 with an average value of approximately €8000 per year. At that point, cash payments within the household decrease rapidly until age 58, level off until age 78 and finally start to decline again from around age 80. Private transfer inflows peak at age 14, when an average child receives resources worth €10,700 per year from the family, and then fall rapidly. Private transfer inflows are fairly constant between ages 27 and 55. Inflows then

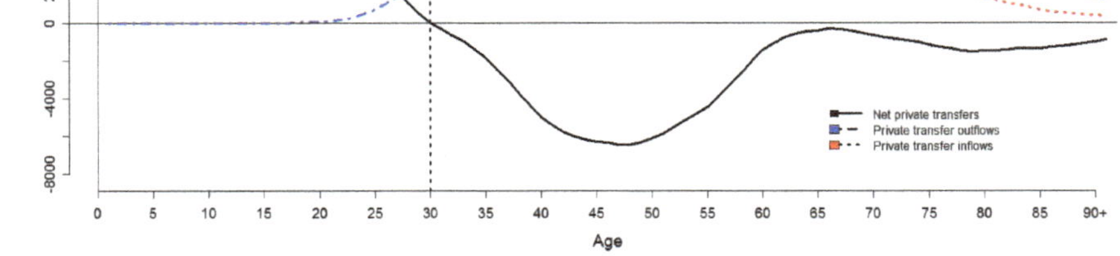

Fig. 3.12 Per capita age profiles of private transfers. *Source* Author's elaborations on Eurostat (2008a, b, c), Istat (2008a, 2009) and various other sources

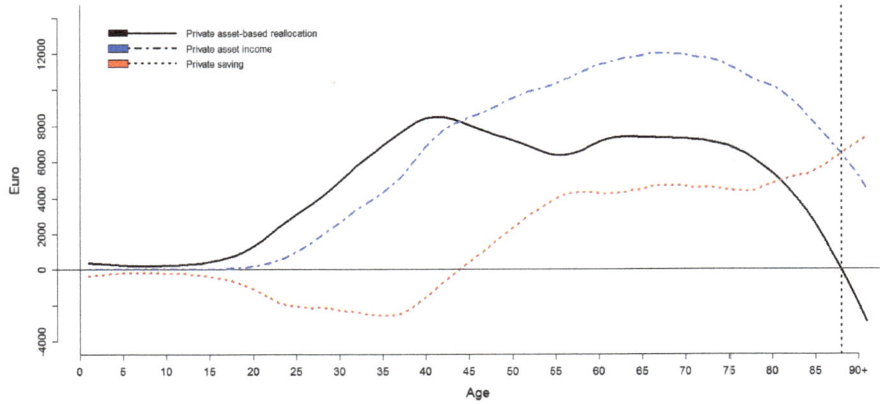

Fig. 3.13 Per capita age profiles of private asset-based reallocations. *Source* Author's elaborations on Eurostat (2008a), Istat (2009), Banca d'Italia (2008)

start to increase and form a bulge up to age 65. Finally, from age 66 and over, private transfer inflows gradually decrease. Nevertheless, net transfers do not turn positive, meaning that individuals continue to be net givers of transfers within the family, even at the oldest ages.

Asset income (Fig. 3.13) rises with age from the mid-twenties, reaching a maximum just past the age of 65, corresponding with retirement, and then decreases. The age schedule of asset income appears to be broadly consistent with the lifecycle hypothesis of saving that assumes individuals build up assets from their earliest working age years to fund their consumption during retirement (Ando and Modigliani 1963). On the other hand, savings become clearly positive only after age 45 and then show an increasing trend with age, consistent with the argument that the mature ages rely heavily on transfers and very little on assets in contexts like Italy, where public programs are generous (Lee and Mason 2011).

3.7 How Italy Finances the Lifecycle Deficit

Figure 3.14 shows a complete picture of the economic lifecycle and the intergenerational reallocation system in Italy in 2008. The market LCD of Italian children lasting until age 26 is supported 60% by private transfers, 32% by public transfers, and 8% through asset-based reallocations, meaning that families play the fundamental role in supporting children. The middle years from 28 to 58 display a similar pattern; labor income is enough to finance these individuals' own consumption and to generate an LCS that is used as an outflow in the form of transfers and/or savings. Adults in middle age reallocate their surplus to deficit ages for the most part through public transfers and to a lesser but still significant extent through private transfers. On the other hand, the LCD in the mature years is financed mainly

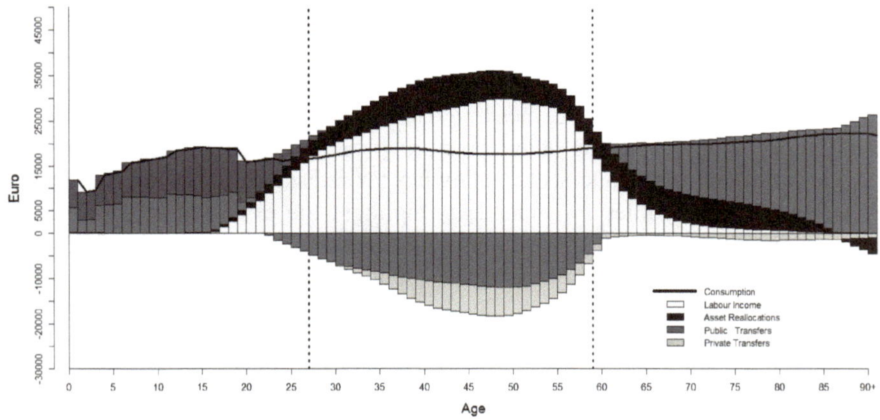

Fig. 3.14 The age reallocation system, Italy 2008. *Source* Author's elaborations on Eurostat (2008a, b, c, d), Istat (2008a, 2009), Banca d'Italia (2008)

by public transfers (67%); 28% consists of asset-based reallocations and only 5% takes the form of private transfers. It is significant that, for these age groups, public transfers in the form of pensions added to their already available economic resources in labor income and asset flows give rise to a small amount of surplus, which is transferred within the family.

Public and private transfers represent the most interesting aspect of the analysis of intergenerational economic equity, since their incidence provides us with important information about Italy's social structure. The comparison between net per capita private and public transfers (Fig. 3.15) highlights the existence of similar age patterns and amounts transferred during young and middle ages. Net public transfers for the young component of the population are positive until age 20, while

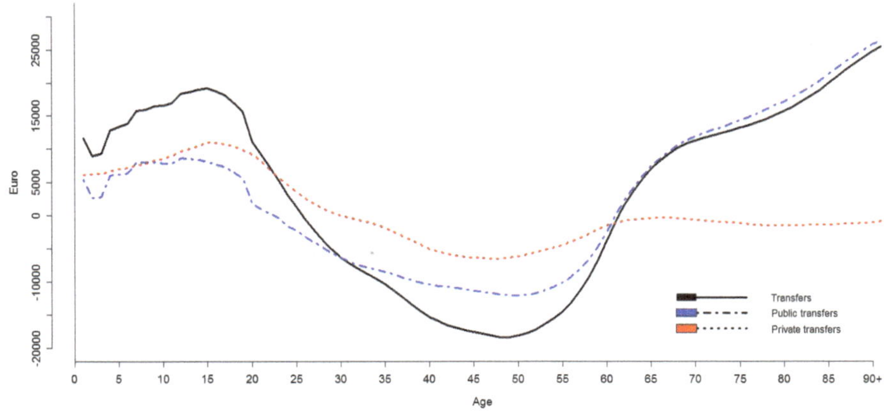

Fig. 3.15 Net per capita age profiles of private and public transfers. *Source* Author's elaborations on Eurostat (2008a, b, c), Istat (2008a, 2009), Banca d'Italia (2008)

within the family the young are net beneficiaries up to age 30. Although people begin to contribute earlier through the state than within the family, net public transfers turn positive around age 60, while private ones remain negative through the remainder of the life course, meaning that people continue to be on average net contributors. As highlighted above, mature people receive a large amount of resources through the public sector, allowing for redistribution within the family. Hence, per capita profiles for older ages highlight the existence of significantly different age patterns for the public and private sectors. In addition to their diverse directions, public transfers grow extremely rapidly with age, while private transfers are almost constant.

3.8 Concluding Remarks

The cross-sectional picture of the Italian economic lifecycle and intergenerational reallocation system has highlighted the existence of fairly high economic dependence among the young and mature population, who are supported by their own households and the state, respectively. The age borders of economic dependence based on the actual age patterns of consumption and labor income—ages 0–26 for the younger group and 59+ for the older component—differ significantly from those conventionally used in demography.

The integrated analysis of the intergenerational support system for the public and private institutional sectors has confirmed the existence of distinctly downward and upward directions of public and private transfers, respectively. The detailed analysis of transfers received from the state by individuals at different ages shows a bias of the public transfer system toward old age pensions, together with a lack of public resources addressed to the specific social needs and risks of prime-age adults (e.g., housing, unemployment, family allowances, etc.). This arrangement can be considered doubly biased, since not only are the needs of young adult and middle ages largely unsupported, but the fiscal burden is also sustained largely through their efforts. However, generous pension programs allow the mature segment of the population to redistribute financial resources within the family, resulting in what is often considered the perverse redistributive paradox of the Italian welfare system. Results for the support system at young ages highlight the existence of a prolonged economic dependence of children sustained by families.

The design of the Italian welfare system raises concerns about both the sustainability and the equity of the underlying intergenerational contract. Future pensioner cohorts are unlikely to experience the present cohorts' levels of lifetime assets, either through individual initiative (work and savings) or through the public redistributive function. Increasingly unstable and poorer families will reduce their abilities to sustain the young. The familiarization of intergenerational obligations toward the young raises questions about the sustainability and equity of the Italian welfare system, and the role of families in providing social welfare for adult children may facilitate the reproduction of social inequalities. Working age adults may be economically squeezed by financial transfers through both the state and the family. Data on individual subjective perceptions would help to evaluate the efficiency of the Italian redistributive system in terms of the well-being of the population, which identifies a promising new avenue of research for the future. Finally, the intergenerational support system cannot be fully understood without taking into consideration gender relations along with the intergenerational interaction, as the next chapter demonstrates.

References

Albertini, M., Kohli, M., & Vogel, C. (2007). Intergenerational transfers of time and money in European families: Common—different regimes? *Journal of European Social Policy, 17*(4), 319–334.

Ando, A., & Modigliani, F. (1963). The "life cycle" hypothesis of saving: Aggregate implications and tests. *The American Economic Review, 53*(1), 55–84.

Auerbach, A. J., Gokhale, J., & Kotlikoff, L. J. (1994). Generational accounting: A meaningful way to evaluate fiscal policy. *The Journal of Economic Perspectives, 8*(1), 73–94.

Barr, N. A. (2001). *The welfare state as piggy bank: Information, risk, uncertainty, and the role of the state*. Oxford: Oxford University Press.

Bengtson, V. L., & Achenbaum, W. A. (Eds.). (1993). *The changing contract across generations*. Piscataway, NJ: Transaction Publishers.

Bloom, D. E., Canning, D., & Fink, G. (2010). Implications of population ageing for economic growth. *Oxford Review of Economic Policy, 26*(4), 583–612.

Esping-Andersen, G., Myles, J., & Smeeding, T. M. (2009). The welfare state and redistribution. In W. Salvedra, B. Nolan, & T. Smeeding (Eds.), *Handbook on economic inequality* (pp. 639–664). Oxford: Oxford University Press.

Hammer, B., Prskawetz, A., & Freund, I. (2015). Production activities and economic dependency by age and gender in Europe: A cross-country comparison. *The Journal of the Economics of Ageing, 5,* 86–97.

Hills, J. (2004). *Inequality and the State*. Oxford: Oxford University Press.

Kuznets, S. (1934). National income 1929–1932: Letter from the Acting Secretary of Commerce. https://fraser.stlouisfed.org/scribd/?title_id=971&filepath=/files/docs/publications/natincome_1934/19340104_nationalinc.pdf. Accessed December 4, 2016.

Lee, R., & Mason, A. (2011). *Population aging and the generational economy: A global perspective*. Northampton, MA: Edward Elgar Publishing.

Mejía-Guevara, I. (2011). The economic lifecycle and intergenerational redistribution in Mexico. In R. Lee & A. Mason (Eds.), *Population aging and the generational economy* (pp. 283–296). Northampton, MA: Edward Elgar Publishing.

Mushkin, S. (1962). Health as an investment. *Journal of Political Economy, 70*(5, Part 2), 129–157.

Samuelson, P. A. (1958). An exact consumption-loan model of interest with or without the social contrivance of money. *The Journal of Political Economy, 66*(6), 467–482.

Stiglitz, J. E., Sen, A., & Fitoussi, J. P. (2009). The measurement of economic performance and social progress revisited: reflections and overview. Report by the Commission on the Measurement of economic Performance and Social Progress. http://govindnair.pbworks.com/w/file/fetch/60985790/Stiglitz_Sen_fitoussi%20report.pdf. Accessed December 4, 2016.

United Nations. (1953). *A system of national accounts and supporting tables*. Studies in methods, Series F, no. 2, rev. 1. New York: United Nations.

United Nations. (1993). *A system of national accounts*. New York: United Nations.

United Nations. (2011). *World population prospects: The 2010 revision*. New York: United Nations.
United Nations. (2013). *National transfer accounts manual: Measuring and analysing the generational economy*. New York: United Nations. http://www.ntaccounts.org/doc/repository/NTA%20manual%202013.pdf. Accessed December 4, 2016.
Vanioli, A. (2014). National accounting at the beginning of the 21st century: Wherefrom? Whereto? *Eurostat Review on National Accounts and Macroeconomic Indicators, 1*, 9–38.
Walker, A. (1996). *The new generational contract*. London: UCL Press.
Preston, S. H. (1984). Children and the elderly: Divergent paths for America's dependents. *Demography, 21*(4), 435–457.

Statistical Sources

Banca d'Italia. (2008). Indagine sui bilanci delle famiglie italiane.
Eurostat. (2008a). Annual sector accounts. http://ec.europa.eu/eurostat/web/sector-accounts/data/database. Accessed December 28, 2016.
Eurostat. (2008b). Government finance statistics, annual government statistics, final consumption expenditure of households by consumption purpose (COICOP). https://data.europa.eu/euodp/it/data/dataset/E3td1eJcpRfbHOtLntXwA. Accessed December 28, 2016.
Eurostat. (2008c). Government finance statistics, annual government statistics, general government expenditure by function (COFOG). http://appsso.eurostat.ec.europa.eu/nui/show.do?dataset=gov_a_exp&lang=en. Accessed December 28, 2016.
Eurostat. (2008d). European system of integrated social protection statistics (ESSPROS). http://ec.europa.eu/eurostat/statistics-explained/index.php/Social_protection_statistics. Accessed December 28, 2016.
Istat. (2008a). Indagine sui consumi delle famiglie.
Istat. (2008b). Multiscopo sulle famiglie: condizioni di salute e ricorso ai servizi sanitari.
Istat. (2009). Indagine sulle condizioni di vita.

Chapter 4
Women Work, Time Transfers, and Informal Welfare

Abstract Drawing on the NTA approach, this chapter conducts an analysis of the Italian economic lifecycle and age reallocation system with a focus on gender and the non-market dimension of the economy. The results highlight the existence of reverse gender patterns in market and non-market production and transfers along the life course. Ultimately, the intergenerational contract is confirmed to be dependent on a gender contract. The combination of paid and unpaid work for women in the middle years raises concerns about the equity and sustainability of the gender contract. Results for the support system for the young show that overall familial transfers in both cash and time contribute to finance more than 50% of children's LCD, the percentage increases to 80% for those between ages 0 and 3. Time transfers are particularly relevant for toddlers. Public care provision for the youngest children, especially nursery service, is identified as a key area of intervention to lighten the load of intergenerational obligations for women.

4.1 Introduction

Since 2010, the idea that a full picture of the intergenerational reallocation system is impossible without the inclusion of the non-market and the gender dimensions has started to gain ground within the NTA community. Pioneering research for the development of a theoretical model of intergenerational transfers incorporating time use had been presented by Lee and Lapkoff (1988). The mantle was then taken up by Phananiramai (2011), who extended the NTA framework to incorporate the age profiles of time transfers for Thailand. Finally, a comprehensive methodology was first developed by Donehower and Mejia-Guevara (2012) and then revised by Donehower (2014) in order to disaggregate SNA quantities by age and gender, thus developing a gender-specific NTA, and to develop a corresponding account for non-market activities named the National Time Transfer Accounts (NTTA). The novelty of the NTTA is twofold. First, the NTTA introduces age and gender into traditional measures of unpaid domestic work developed by the Household Satellite Accounts approach by splitting the value of household labor among gender and age

M. Zannella, *The Economic Lifecycle, Gender and Intergenerational Support*, SpringerBriefs in Population Studies, DOI 10.1007/978-3-319-62669-7_4

groups. Second, the NTTA moves beyond the traditional focus on the value of domestic work by estimating the consumption, in addition to the production, of the time required to generate services and goods within the household. Combining NTA and NTTA estimates by age and gender provides us with better measures of familial and women's contributions to the economy and thus corrects the gender bias of the NTA and indeed of any accounting or analytical system limited to the public sector or aggregates of national accounts. As a result, the understanding of the formal and informal intergenerational reallocation system is significantly broadened.

Recently, the NTA working group on gender and time use made efforts to develop a comparative NTTA to bring women's economic contributions into the view of society and policymakers as well as to analyze intercountry differences in gender patterns of paid and unpaid work during the life course. The development of the NTTA for low- and middle-income countries has been sustained by the NTA research network through the development of the Counting Women's Work project (http://www.cww-dpru.uct.ac.za/about_cww). Comparative NTTA studies for European countries have been developed by Zagheni and Zannella (2013), Zagheni et al. (2014), Hammer et al. (2015), and Varga et al. (2017). Within the AGENTA project (http://www.agenta-project.eu/en/index.htm), Vargha et al. (2016) developed a methodology for the creation of a European NTTA based on publicly available harmonized time use data provided by the Harmonised European Time Use Survey (HETUS) and the Multinational Time Use Study (MTUS). The use of harmonized data and methods has the advantage of allowing for the construction of comparable NTTA sets for 17 European countries (perfect comparability is not possible because the HETUS and MTUS data are not temporally homogeneous across countries). On the other side, methods to estimate the European NTTA are based on the introduction of a greater number of assumptions due to the limited information available from harmonized data sources as compared with national time use data. In this chapter, the methods used to build an NTTA based on the detailed Italian time use survey are discussed.

The chapter is structured as follows. Section 4.2 briefly describes the methods used to estimate a gender-specific NTA. Section 4.3 introduces the concept of a time use survey, describes the structure of the Italian data, and provides a brief overview of harmonized time use data. Section 4.4 introduces general conceptual issues related to the construction of satellite accounts for household production, Sect. 4.5 provides an overview of the NTTA methodology for Italy, and Sects. 4.5.1 and 4.5.2 describe the specific methods implemented for the estimates of sex-specific age profiles of time consumption and transfers. Section 4.6 presents the main results related to the gender-specific NTA for Italy in 2008; Sect. 4.6.1 presents a detailed disaggregation of social protection by gender and age. Section 4.7 reports the results related to the NTTA and Sect. 4.7.1 analyzes unpaid production in time units. Section 4.8 presents results for the total economy by combining NTA and NTTA estimates; Sect. 4.8.1 provides a comprehensive picture of intergenerational and gender transfers within the family and of financing of consumption for LCD ages. Section 4.9 concludes.

4.2 Building National Transfer Satellite Accounts for Gender

Constructing an NTA by gender requires the same data sources and procedures already described in Chap. 2 for traditional NTA estimates, but disaggregating SNA economic activities by gender in addition to age. Indeed, as in the traditional NTA, we use different estimation strategies depending on the nature of the economic activity and the data sources available. It should be recalled that data can be provided by administrative or survey sources. Profiles of public consumption are based mainly on administrative data, whereas those for labor income and private consumption are based on Istat survey microdata from the Statistics on Income and Living Conditions (UDB IT-SILC) (Istat 2009) and the Household Budget Survey (HBS) (Istat 2008a), respectively. Survey microdata can refer to individuals, as in the case of the UDB IT-SILC, or to households, as in the case of the HBS. Individual-level data allow for direct estimates of the profiles as sex- and age-specific averages. On the other hand, household-level data require an additional step; aggregate data at the household level must be allocated to the individual household members through appropriate assumptions. Once data are distributed at the individual level, per capita sex-specific age profiles for private consumption are obtained in the usual way as gender- and age-specific averages. Aggregate age profiles are estimated as the product between per capita age profiles and the corresponding population count.

Finally, sex-specific age profiles must be adjusted in order to ensure their consistency with the SNA, which does not provide economic aggregates detailed by gender. Sex-specific age profiles are adjusted to match the corresponding single-gender age profile, adjusted with SNA data. This ensures that sex- and age-specific estimates are consistent with both age-specific estimates and with SNA macroaggregates. Adjustments are calculated separately for each age group, but are the same for men and women within each age group.

4.3 Time Use Data

Sex-specific age profiles of time production, consumption, and transfers are based on microdata from the most recent Italian time use survey available, for 2008–2009 (Istat 2008b). The survey sample, consisting of 44,606 individuals and 18,250 households, is organized into two levels (municipalities and households) with interviews conducted throughout the year. Typically, a time use survey has a fairly complex structure consisting of three files of data: an individual file, a daily diary, and a weekly diary.

The individual file collects sociodemographic information at the individual level by means of interviews. The individual file has one record for each household member. The daily diary file consists of time data collected through a diary technique; respondents record their time use during the previous 24 h in their own words. Daily diaries are randomly distributed across the days of the week to all households members aged 3 years and above. In the Italian time use survey, all members of a household must fill in their daily diaries on the same day. Diaries provide extremely detailed information on the activities performed during the day, since they are based on a grid of 10-min time intervals with a description of (1) the main activity carried out by the respondent, (2) the possible presence of a secondary or parallel activity, (3) the location, and (4) the possible presence of another person or persons. As a result, the diary data consist of a sequence of episodes or events, each characterized by these four recording domains. The daily dairy files are structured in one record for each episode and contain as many records as the total number of episodes reported by the individuals in the sample. In addition to the daily diary, household members aged 15 years and over are required to fill in a weekly diary with information related to their working time. However, for the purpose of this study, only the individual and daily diary files were used. An individual and a temporal identifier are provided. The individual identifier enables the connection of a specific respondent to a particular diary day and to the background information contained in the individual file. The temporal identifier indicates the starting and ending time of each episode in a diary and is necessary to calculate the duration of each episode.

Starting in the 1990s, Eurostat has conducted efforts in order to foster the comparability of time use statistics at the European level. As a result, HETUS guidelines were first developed in 2000 (Eurostat 2004) and revised in 2008 (Eurostat 2009). The HETUS guidelines contain recommendations for the harmonization of survey design, including aspects related to sample design, data collection, survey forms, and a list of coding activities. However, European countries still vary to different degrees in terms of survey design and timing. A principal difference in the design of the survey regards the creation of national samples; some countries draw on household samples, while others use the individual as the sampling unit. In both cases, socio-demographic information about all members of the sampled households may or may not be recorded. Individual or incomplete sample design creates severe limitations for the analysis of time transfers since, as reported explicitly in the HETUS guidelines, both socio-demographic data and time use data for all household members are needed to enable the analysis of intra-household dependencies. Despite the remaining time use survey design differences, the construction of a database containing comparable time use data for 15 European countries has been made possible. The data are freely downloadable in the form of flexible tables at the HETUS website (https://www.h5.scb.se/tus/tus/). A similar harmonization effort has been developed by Jonathan Gershuny, who developed the MTUS in the 1970s. Originally, the MTUS allowed for comparison of UK time use data with the Multinational Time Budget Study (Szalai 1966) and data from Canada and Denmark. The MTUS now encompasses over 60 data sets from 25 countries (Gershuny and Fisher 2013), including data from the American Time Use Survey (ATUS) and HETUS (see Fisher 2015).

4.4 Selecting and Pricing Home Production Activities: General Conceptual Issues

The first step in building an NTTA consists of identifying the relevant time use survey productive household activities. For this purpose, I selected a set of activities that meet the third party criterion (Reid 1934), i.e., those household activities with a market substitute for the time of the household members. Specifically, I selected food management, household upkeep, creating and caring for textiles, gardening and pet care, construction and repairs, shopping and services, household management, child care, help to an adult household member, informal help to other households, and travel related to household care, such as trips for shopping, services, and child care.

In a second step, the selected activities must be priced in order to be comparable with NTA estimates and with economic activities reported in the SNA. To this end, different methods can be used. A first methodological consideration regards the evaluation of home production using an input or output method. The input method values the home production by imputing a cost (or wage) to the time devoted to productive activities. Meanwhile, the output method values home production by imputing a value to the resulting quantity of goods or services produced. For example, cooking a meal for the family is valued as the number of the hours spent cooking times the imputed cost for the activity using the input method and as the quantity of the meal produced times its imputed cost with the output method. The output method has the advantage of allowing differences in productivity and economies of scale to be taken into account.

However, in most cases the output method cannot be applied, since no data tell us how much of a product is created by performing domestic activities, and we do not have information about the other inputs of production other than time that are used to contribute to form the final price of the product, such as purchased materials and service from consumer durables. For example, in the case of cooking a meal, the amount of time spent on the activity can be derived from time use survey data, but that data does not report any information about any food purchased or household appliances involved in preparing the meal. Thus, the input approach is used in this study, as in most studies in the field, in order to value household production.

A second methodological consideration regards the choice of a criterion to impute a wage to productive home activities. Two main criteria are used in the literature, the opportunity cost and the replacement cost. The opportunity cost approach assigns the wage to the person who performed the activity. Thus, time devoted to wash dishes is priced differently when the person performing the activity is a professional versus an unskilled worker. The replacement cost approach prices the activity at its corresponding wage in the market, so that the monetary value of an activity is the same for all the individuals that perform. Replacement cost can be divided into general and specialist replacement costs. All domestic activities are priced with the same wage calculated as the average wage of a domestic worker when using the general replacement method, whereas the specialist replacement method assigns each activity the corresponding specific wage in the market, so that preparing a meal is priced at the market wage of a cook, doing laundry is priced at the market wage of a laundress, etc. The opportunity cost method can overestimate household production, especially when performed by men, who typically have higher market wages than women. Therefore, the specialized replacement method is used to assign monetary values to household production activities.

4.5 Building the National Time Transfer Accounts

The NTTA relies on the same logic as the NTA, with two main differences; age reallocations occur only in the form of private transfers, i.e., intra- and inter-household transfers, given that the state cannot directly transfer time and no time savings are possible. Thus, the economic identity in Chap. 2 can be rewritten as follows:

$$\underbrace{C(x) - P(x)}_{LCD.or.LCS} = \underbrace{\tau^{+}(x) - \tau^{-}(x)}_{Transfers}, \tag{4.1}$$

where x is age; C is consumption, P is production, and t^{+} and t^{-} are transfers made and received, respectively.

Sex-specific age profiles of household production can be estimated directly from survey microdata as the average time dedicated to the selected activities by sex and age. On the other hand, time use surveys do not report any information on how the time produced by an individual in the household is consumed by other household members. However, the laws of physics tell us that time cannot be accumulated in the form of savings for the future; as a logical consequence, the time produced within the household must be consumed entirely by the household members. However, it is not always easy to identify the beneficiaries of different household productive activities.

First, we must distinguish between general and targeted activities. The production of general activities is not explicitly targeted to any specific individual and could be consumed by any member of the household. For example, if the time use survey data report cooking a meal, we do not know whether that meal is cooked for the cook's own consumption or also for that of other household members. In the second case, we cannot allocate shares of the cooking time as transfers to each household member without knowing exactly who eats which meals. Conversely, care of children and adults are by definition targeted to individuals within specific age groups, those aged 0–17 and adults aged 18 and above, respectively. Here, limited information about the beneficiaries of the activity is available; the producer of the care activity is by definition excluded from its consumption and the broad age groups of the recipients are known. In single-child households, of course, all the time producing child care activities is automatically assigned to the consumption of that one child. Similarly, in households that consist only of two adults, any time producing adult care by one adult is automatically assigned to the consumption of the other. On the other hand, imputing the production of child or adult care to its consumption is not straightforward and requires the introduction of assumptions in the case of households with more than one child or two adults.

In principle, assigning the production of domestic activities to the consumption of each individual in the household would require basic information about the household's structure. As noted above, the Italian time use survey collects socio-demographic information for all household members. However, this is not the case for every time use survey at the European level, despite Eurostat recommendations in that regard (Eurostat 2009). Methods used to derive the age and gender schedules of time consumption vary significantly, depending on the information available from a given time use survey. Countries for which the household structure is not available from the data must estimate consumption profiles directly at the population level by introducing a number of simplifying assumptions as, for example, equal shares of consumption (see Vargha et al. 2016 for more details). Having full socio-demographic information available for Italy makes it possible to proceed with more detailed estimates by allocating, in a first step, time production to individual consumption within the household and, then, estimating sex-specific age profiles as the corresponding averages for the population.

4.5.1 Time Consumption

An homogeneous linear model is used to estimate individual consumption within the household. The regression method relies on the following assumption; time consumption of unpaid domestic work depends both on the number and ages of household members, although time consumption is assumed to be independent of gender. The total time produced or consumed for domestic activities by a household j (C_j) can be expressed as a linear function of the number of its components (N_j) by age x. The model has no intercept since all the time produced is consumed within the household; it distinguishes between general and targeted activities by introducing flexible age limits (a and b) varying according with the nature of the considered activity:

$$C_j = \sum_{x=a}^{b} \alpha(x) \cdot N_j(x), \tag{4.2}$$

where $a = 0$ and $b = 90+$ for general activities, $a = 0$ and $b = 17$ for child care, $a = 18$ and $b = 90+$ for adult care; C_j = total time for the domestic activities produced/consumed by the household j, $N_j(x)$ = the number of members aged x in the household j, and $\alpha(x)$ are the parameters to be estimated. Parameter estimates are used as weights to assign the production of activities within the household to the consumption of its members by age. Hence, sex-specific age profiles of consumption by typology of activity are estimated as the corresponding weighted average values[1] over all households. Coefficients are smoothed for each single-year age group using Friedman's Super Smoother (Friedman 1984).

4.5.2 Time Transfers

The difference between consumption and production provides a measure of the LCD or LCS of time. Any time surplus is entirely transferred since no time savings are possible. As with monetary transfers, time transfers (i) include intra-household transfers and inter-household transfers and (ii) can be divided into outflows (the time transferred to other individuals) and inflows (time received from other individuals).

As regards inter-household time transfers, the age and gender schedule of time production for informal help to other households is taken as an outflow for the person performing the activity and the corresponding sex-specific age profiles of consumption are taken as an inflow for individuals benefiting from the activity.

Intra-household time transfers for age-targeted activities like child care and adult care behave similarly to inter-household transfers; sex-specific age profiles of time produced and consumed for care activities are taken as an outflow for the person providing care and as an inflow for the person receiving care, respectively. Estimates of intra-household time transfer outflows for general activities, given their intrinsic nature, require a further step in order to subtract the portion of time produced for self-consumption. For example, if one person spends one hour of time cleaning the house, then his or her outflow for this activity is equal to one hour minus the proportion of their own time consumption given by the age weight derived by the parameters estimates in Eq. (4.2).

4.6 National Transfer Accounts by Gender: Main Results

The results of the economic lifecycle for women (Fig. 4.1a) and men (Fig. 4.1b) highlight the existence of significant gender differences. During the early years of life, consumption exceeds labor income until age 24 for men and age 36 for women. Men's LCS begins at age 25 and ends at age 60, lasting 35 years in total, whereas the LCS of women covers ages 37–55, for a total duration of 18 years. As a result, on average, actual old-age dependency starts at age 61 for men and age 56 for women. The LCS of men and women differs not only with regard to age borders but

[1]Sample weights are used to reproduce the demographic structure of the Italian population.

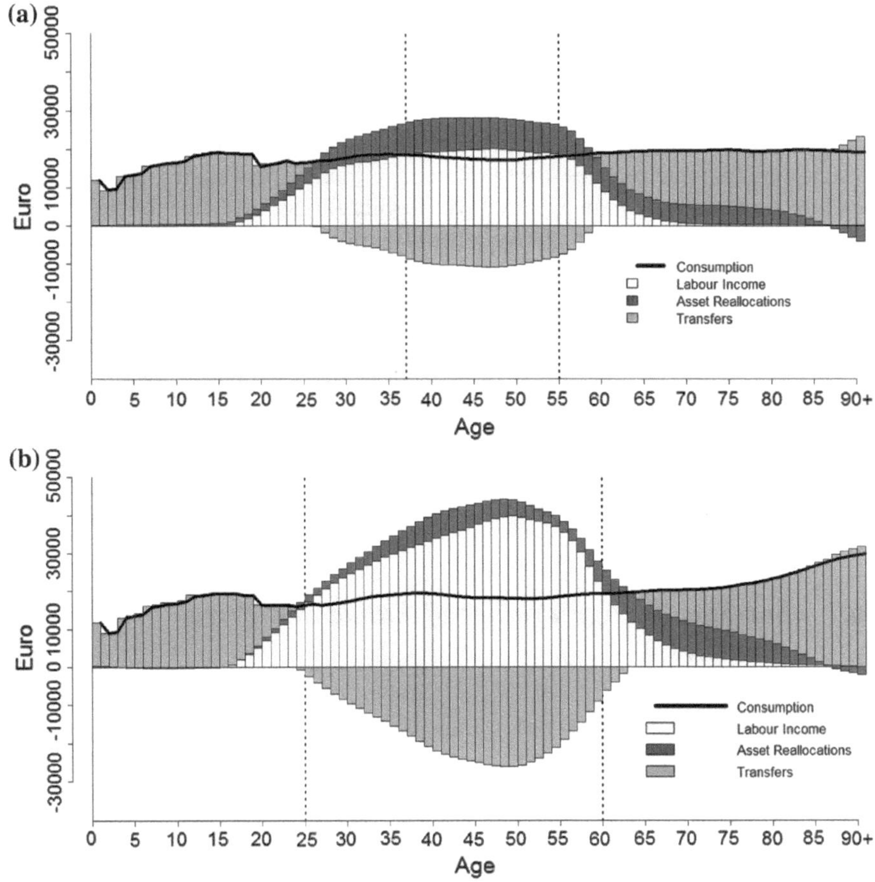

Fig. 4.1 **a** Per capita age profile of economic lifecycle and reallocation (women), market economy. **b** Per capita age profile of economic lifecycle and reallocations (men), market economy. *Source* Author's elaborations on Eurostat (2008a, b, c, d), Istat (2008a; 2009), Banca d'Italia (2008) and various other sources

also to the levels, with women generating significantly lower values of surplus than men.

Gender differences in the economic lifecycle are explained largely by the labor income component; according to Eurostat, Italy has the second lowest female employment rate in Europe (2014) with less than half of the active female population participating in the labor market. Labor income starts to rise earlier for men than for women and increases rapidly with age, peaking at 49 years of age with a value of €40,000. Women, meanwhile, show considerably lower levels and a rather flat age pattern of labor income during most of their working lives, with a maximum value of €20,000—or half that of men—reached at 47 years. Gender differences also persist during the latest stages of the lifecycle; men's labor income at mature ages lasts longer than women's, as a result of the different levels of self-employment.

Consumption overlaps for men and women at young and middle ages, whereas it starts to behave differently at mature ages, with men and women showing increasing and constant per capita profiles, respectively. Gender differences in consumption at mature ages are explained primarily by higher public health spending for men than women, which will require further investigation using more detailed data based on administrative records on hospital discharges. Differences in the economic lifecycle of men and women are reflected in age reallocations and particularly in profiles of net transfers. Transfers behave similarly for children of both genders, but highlight the existence of significant differences at middle and working ages, with men paying and receiving more than women during working and retirement ages, respectively. In the next section, sex-specific age profiles of net transfers distinguished by institutional sectors—private versus public transfers—are presented in order to understand whether or not gender differences in transfers reveal the existence of similar patterns within the family and the state.

4.6.1 Sex-Specific Age Profiles of Public and Private Transfers

Sex-specific age profiles of net public transfers (Fig. 4.2) overlap for children aged up to 20 years, indicating that they receive the same amount of resources from the state mostly through education and health programs. During working ages, net public transfers are negative for both genders, meaning that they pay more than what they receive from the public sector. Net transfers for men and women turn positive again at mature ages when they start to grow rapidly, largely as a result of retirement pensions. However, the net transfers paid and received during working and mature ages, respectively, are significantly higher for men than for women due to corresponding differences in labor market participation. Thus, with regard to net public transfers at adult ages, men and women show similar qualitative age patterns but important quantitative differences.

Sex-specific age profiles are also similar for male and female children in the case of net private transfers (Fig. 4.3); they are both dependent on older family members to finance their consumption. Then, after age 25, the profiles diverge dramatically. Net private transfers are on average positive for women during virtually the entire life course, with the exception of ages 40–50, when they generate a small amount of positive cash transfers. By contrast, net private transfers turn negative for men from age 26 and remain that way for the rest of their lives. Therefore, with regard to the market economy, adult men and women are on average net contributors and net beneficiaries within the family, respectively. Once again, gender differences within the private sector are explained by differences in labor market participation; higher occupational levels allow men to generate an LCS at middle ages that is at least

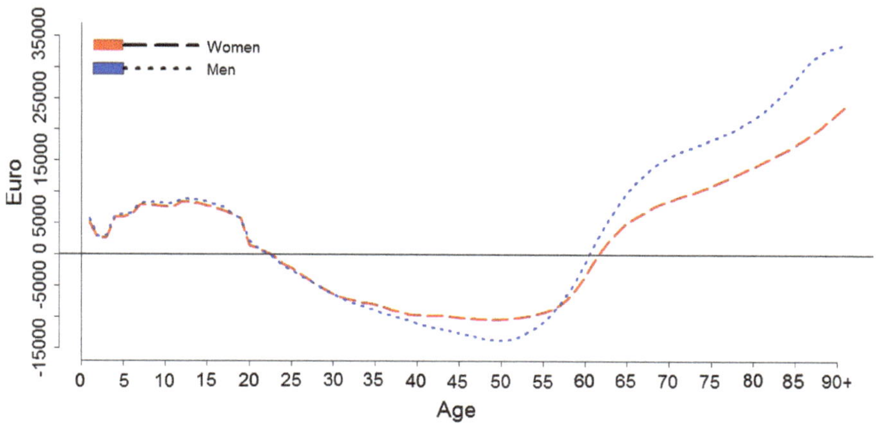

Fig. 4.2 Per capita age profile of public transfers by gender, market economy. *Source* Author's elaborations on Eurostat (2008a, c, d) and various other sources

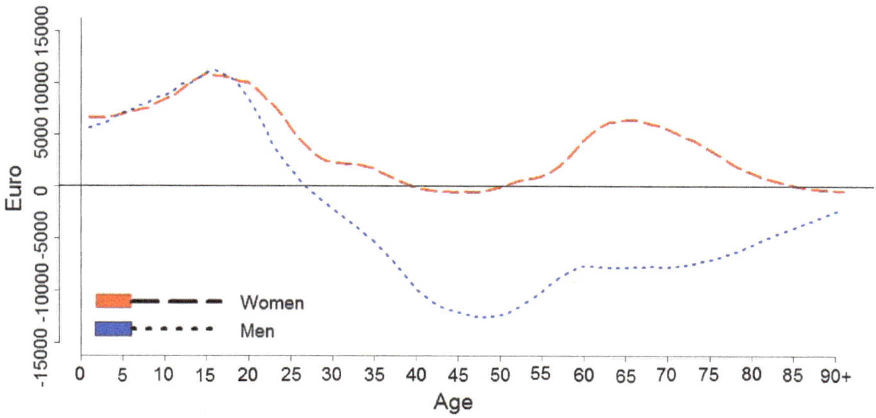

Fig. 4.3 Per capita age profile of private transfers by gender. *Source* Author's elaborations on Eurostat (2008a, b, c), Istat (2008a; 2009), and various other sources

partly transferred to other members of their households. Men's higher occupational levels are also reflected in higher inflows received from the state at older ages in the form of pensions that can be redistributed among family members.

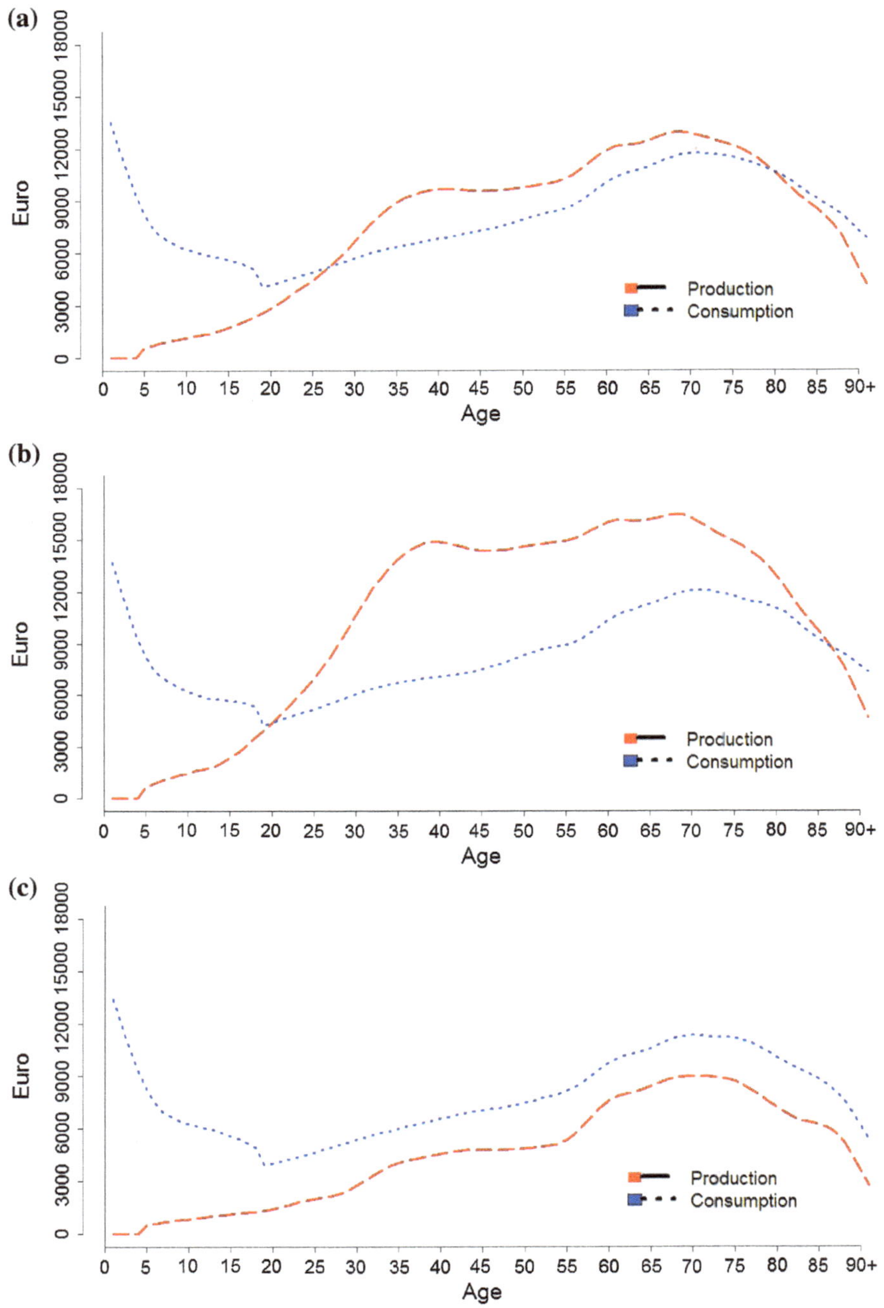

Fig. 4.4 Per capita age profile of economic lifecycle, non-market economy. **a** Both genders, **b** Women, **c** Men. *Source* Author's elaborations on Istat (2008b)

4.7 National Time Transfer Accounts: Primary Results

Age profiles for both genders combined of the non-market economic lifecycle are presented in Fig. 4.4a.[2] Like the market-based economic lifecycle, children experience an LCD from ages 0 through 26, consuming more domestic time than they produce and thus requiring time transfers from older members of the family in order to have their needs met. Non-market consumption at young ages behave similar to its market equivalent; it is significantly high for newborns until the age of three with a corresponding market value of more than €12,000 per year. At that point, time consumption falls rapidly with age and stays constant with an average value of about €6500 per year during the primary school years. However, non-market consumption reveals the existence of distinctive features compared to market consumption during the adult years; it increases steadily during adult ages and rises at retirement ages, when people on average spend more time at home. Finally, it declines at older ages, primarily as an effect of changing household structures.

Non-market production, which is estimated in total to represent 29% of Italian GDP in 2008, highlights the existence of significant qualitative differences when compared to labor income. First, production starts earlier in the non-market economy due to the help provided by children in domestic activities and, most probably, to time-reporting issues. For example, an activity such as playing to help parents with domestic chores may be reported as domestic work instead of playing in time diaries. More importantly, the age pattern of non-market production is not U-shaped, as it is for labor income, but shows a distinctive M-shape. The M-shape curve of non-market production is characterized by two bulges that correspond to the main stages of the life course: the childbearing and retirement stages. Finally, in the non-market economy, people also continue to produce at mature ages, as time production exceeds time consumption through age 78. Thus, people have on average an LCS of 52 years in the non-market economy.

However, looking at sex-specific age profiles of non-market consumption and production reveals the existence of dramatically different situations between genders (Fig. 4.4b, c). Even at young ages, female children contribute more to domestic chores than their male peers. Results for younger ages suggest the existence of a cultural influence on the division of unpaid domestic work; both male and female children are involved in compulsory education, so gender differences at this stage of life cannot be explained by different decisions regarding time allocation to productive activities. Afterward, female production grows very rapidly until it

[2]NTTA estimates presented in this chapter may show some differences from those that can be found in a previous article (Zannella 2014) due to some adjustments in the data and methods used. Estimates presented in this chapter do not include time use activities performed simulataneously. All family members should fill in the diary on the same day. For this reason, micro-data has been corrected to eliminate the influence of diaries that have been compiled on different days from members of the same family. Difference in NTTA estimates are reflected also in those for the toal economy.

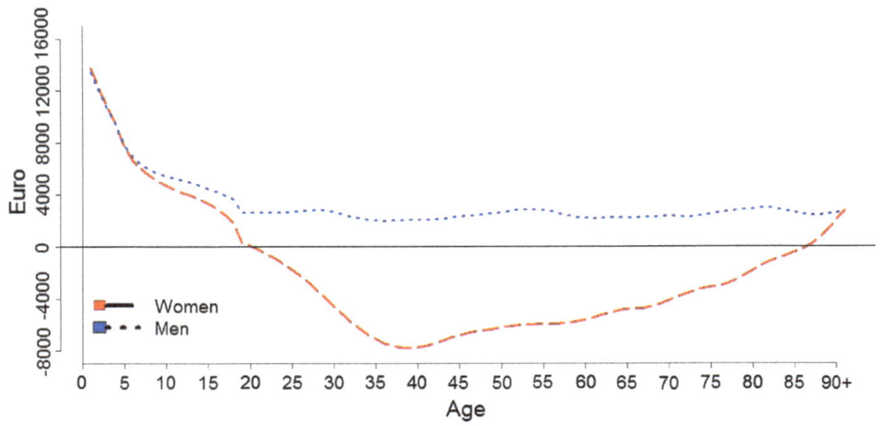

Fig. 4.5 Per capita age profile of transfers by gender, non-market economy. *Source* Author's elaborations on Istat (2008b)

reaches its first bulge, between ages 30 and 40, before subsequently stabilizing at very high levels during virtually all of their remaining years. On the other hand, men increase their production with age less significantly and at a slower pace until retirement. As a result, the production curve of men is less M-shaped with a moderate first bulge at middle ages and a more pronounced bulge during in the mature years.

The presence for both genders of a bulge between ages 30 and 40, although it is significantly larger for women than for men, is a common result in comparative studies on gender differences in time allocation, highlighting the enormous impact of a young child or children on parental time dedicated to household chores and child care activities (Zagheni et al. 2015). Women's contribution to household production at childbearing ages appears to be particularly significant for Italian women; female per capita non-market production between ages 30 and 40 represents 51% of per capita GDP, which is five percentage points above the European average (Vargha et al. 2016). Time use studies have shown that as a household's children grow older, especially after reaching school age, adult females tend gradually to reduce the time devoted to unpaid domestic work and to increase the time spent on market work (Apps and Rees 2005). However, this is not the case in Italy, where age profiles of market and non-market work do not present significant changes during the life course; labor income does not experience a significant recovery and household production continues to show very high values. Results in line with those reported for Italy in Anxo et al. (2007) suggest the existence of a strong gender specialization and the predominance of families oriented toward a male-breadwinner social organization.

As noted above, the difference between consumption and production in the non-market economy (i.e., the LCD or LCS of time) provides a measure of net transfers, since no other form of reallocation exists, because it is not possible to save time and the state cannot directly transfer time to individuals or households. The LCD of women (Fig. 4.5) becomes an LCS at age 20, indicating that they are producing more time than they need to satisfy their own domestic needs. The average age at which consumption again exceeds production and generates an LCD is 85 years for women. By contrast, men's production never exceeds their consumption, meaning that men have a non-market LCD throughout their entire lives. In a study based on time use data for 17 European countries,[3] Vargha et al. (2016) report that European men are on average net contributors from approximately ages 30 to 50. However, Fig. 4.5 shows that this is not true in Italy, where men have positive net time transfers at all ages. By contrast, beginning at age 20 and during virtually the entire remainder of the life course, women are net providers of time transfers to men and younger household members. It is thus possible to assert the existence of a reverse gender pattern between the market and non-market segments of the economy. Women have a market surplus that allows them, at a minimum, to finance their own consumption for a substantial portion of their lives, which is not true for men in the non-market economy, in which they remain dependent upon women to make up their deficits.

4.7.1 Household Production in Time Units

Table 4.1 reports the relative composition of women's and men's non-market work by detailed activities and the corresponding average time, measured in hours per week, dedicated to each activity. The composition of domestic time reveals the

Table 4.1 Household and family care, percentage composition, and per capita weekly hours by gender

Detailed household production activities	Percentage composition			Per capita (hours per week)		
	Both	Men	Women	Both	Men	Women
Household and Family Care	**100.0**	**100.0**	**100.0**	**29.4**	**18.7**	**39.4**
Food Management	43.3	44.1	43.0	12.7	8.3	17.0
Household Upkeep	18.7	9.2	22.9	5.5	1.7	9.0
Making and Care of Textiles	5.5	0.3	7.8	1.6	0.1	3.1
Gardening and Pet Care	5.0	11.6	2.1	1.5	2.2	0.8
Construction and Repairs	0.7	2.2	0.1	0.2	0.4	0.0
Shopping and Services	10.0	12.4	8.9	2.9	2.3	3.5
Household Management	0.3	0.5	0.1	0.1	0.1	0.1
Child Care	5.7	5.1	6.0	1.7	1.0	2.4
Help for an Adult Family Member	3.9	5.5	3.2	1.1	1.0	1.2
Travel Related to Household Care	6.9	9.1	5.9	2.0	1.7	2.3

Source Author's elaborations on Istat (2008b)

[3]The study is based on HETUS data.

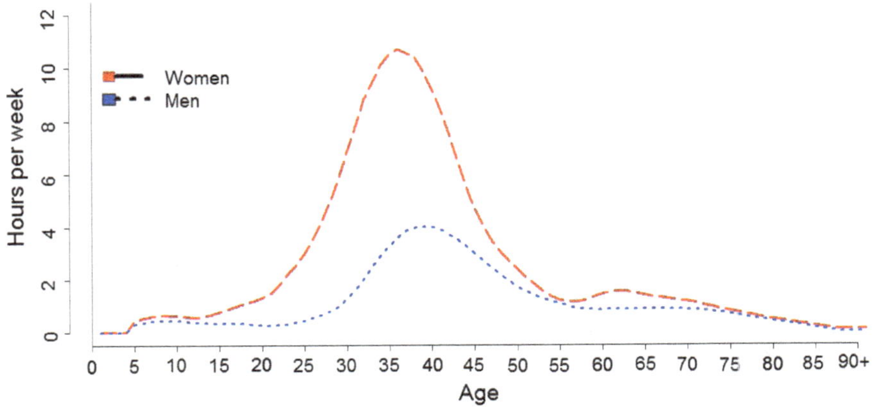

Fig. 4.6 Per capita age profile of child care production by genders (hours per week). *Source* Author's elaborations on Istat (2008b)

existence of some similarities between genders; cooking is the most relevant activity for both men and women (representing 44.1 and 43.0% of total domestic time, respectively) and men and women devote similar shares of time to child care (5.1 and 6.0% of their total time for household production, respectively). However, women spend on average twice as much time as men for cooking and two and half times more hours on child care. A number of activities reveal a strong degree of specialization; women bear the main responsibility for household upkeep and care for textiles, to which they devote considerably higher time per capita than men. Meanwhile, men are mainly responsible for gardening, pet care, and construction and repairs, the only activities for which men report both a higher share and longer average hours than women. Finally, men devote a greater share of their total domestic work time but fewer numerical hours per week on shopping and services than women.

However, aggregate numbers for men and women provide an incomplete picture of non-market work, since time use studies make clear that time allocated to household production varies considerably over the life course. Figure 4.6 presents a detailed analysis by age and gender of the time dedicated to the highly age-sensitive activity of child care. On average, child care starts to grow rapidly for women starting from their 20s and exceeds 10 hours per week between approximately ages 30 and 40;[4] while the curve is shifted to the left for men, who devote a maximum of 4 hours per week to child care around age 40. Strikingly, child care continues into the mature years for both genders due to caring for grandchildren. Even so, grand-parenting is more evident for women between approximately ages 60 and 75. Small amounts of child care are also observed among children at young ages, likely due to time spent with siblings.

[4]It should be recalled that the profiles are calculated as population averages by age and gender and hence include both parents and individuals without children.

4.8 Total Economy

This section discusses the results for the total economy, i.e., the combination of market and non-market activities, and provides a comprehensive cross-sectional picture of the economic relationships between Italian generations and genders in 2008. Adding non-market to market activities has two main effects on the economic lifecycle of men and women combined. First, it raises levels of consumption and particularly of consumption by preschool children and those at mature ages (Fig. 4.7a). Second, it affects both the quantitative levels and the qualitative shape of production by increasing its per capita values at virtually all ages and by shifting forward the right tail of its curve by extending the upper age limits of productive activities. In aggregate terms, non-market production raises the value of the total output of the economy from approximately 830 to 1.313 billion euros, an increase of 58.2% over estimates for the market economy alone. With regard to total population, the levels of surplus and deficit change significantly with the inclusion of unpaid domestic work but the age borders at which the deficits become surpluses and vice versa remain rather constant. The inclusion of the non-market economy raises the value of the youth deficit (compared to that in the market economy) by 26.4%, while the economic dependence among those of mature age decreases by 4.9% (Table 4.2). However, further disaggregation of results for the total economy by gender reveals the existence of key differences in the economic lifecycle of men and women. The period during which production exceeds consumption is extended by 13 years for women (Fig. 4.7b). In the market economy, women are on average able to finance their own consumption between ages 37 and 55, for an LCS of 19 years. Adding non-market work to the analysis, though, indicates that women's LCS lasts an average of 32 years, from age 27 to age 60. In aggregate terms, women's overall surplus increases by 95.5% in the total economy as compared to the market-only economy. This increase is explained by a corresponding increase in levels of total production for women; household production more than double female production, raising its value by 120%. By contrast, men (Fig. 4.7c) see a considerable decrease (19.4%) in the aggregate value of their surplus as well as a slight reduction in the temporal length of their LCS, due to their dependency in the non-market economy. Differences between genders are not only found in surplus ages but also in deficit ages. During youth, both female and male children increase their LCDs over the estimates for the market economy. However, the deficit among the young increases to a lesser extent for females (21.1%) than for males (31.4%), due to their earlier contributions to the household economy. As reported above, the deficit during the mature ages for the entire population decreases in the total economy when compared to the market economy. However, men and women differ in this regard; the deficit increases for the former by 14.2% and decreases for the latter by 22.1%.

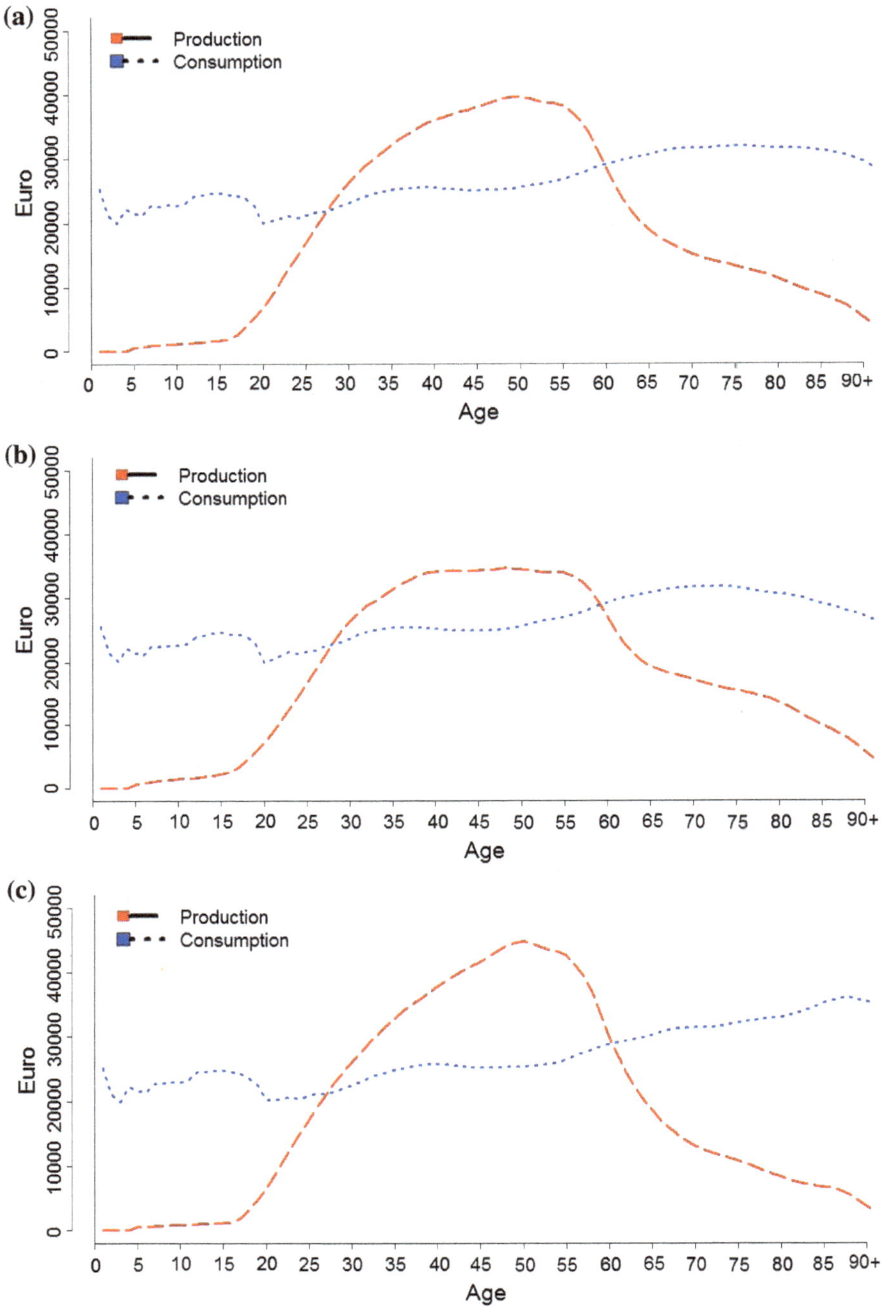

Fig. 4.7 Per capita age profile of production and consumption. **a** Both genders, **b** Women, **c** Men. *Source* Author's elaborations on Eurostat (2008a, b c), Istat (2008a, b; 2009)

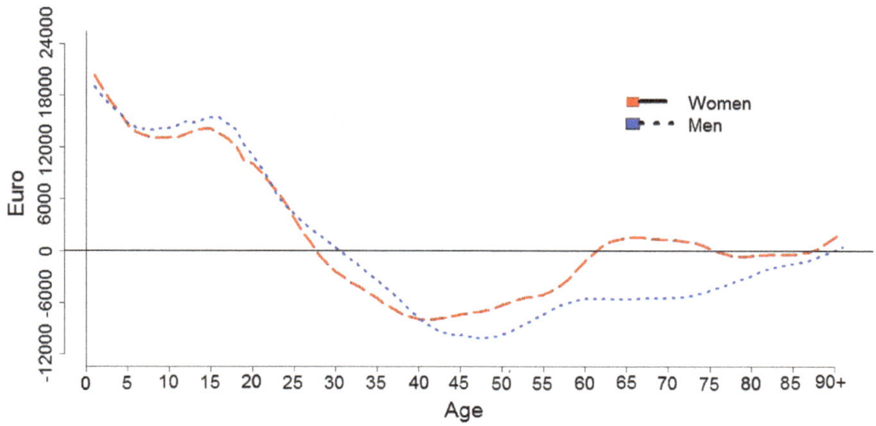

Fig. 4.8 Per capita age profile of private transfers by gender, total economy. *Source* Author's elaborations on Eurostat (2008a, b, c), Istat (2008b; 2009) and various other sources

4.8.1 Reallocation System and Finance of Consumption

Figure 4.8 presents sex-specific age profiles of net private transfers in the total economy. It should be recalled that the inclusion of the non-market economy only has an effect on familial transfers, whereas it leaves public transfers and asset-based reallocations unchanged. Private transfers for young children highlight both quantitative and qualitative differences in the total as compared to the market economy. Children receive significantly larger amounts of transfers in the total economy than in the market economy, as a result of their high levels of non-market consumption. In the total economy, private transfers peak at age 0, when an average newborn receive around €20,000 per year, or more than three times the corresponding transfers received in the market economy. Private transfers then fall rapidly until primary school age is reached, when per capita values stabilize at relatively lower values (around €14,000 per year) during the period of compulsory schooling. Starting from around age five through the early twenties, male children receive slightly more private transfers than their female peers, most likely due to female children's earlier and greater contributions in helping parents (largely mothers) with household chores. Private transfers turn positive at ages 27 and 32 for women and men, respectively. Women provide more transfers compared to men from ages 30 to 40, due to their significant contribution to the household economy in the childbearing years. On the other hand, men's contribution to familial transfers exceeds that of women from around age 40 onward. On average, total private transfers turn positive again for women between ages 60 and 75; at that point, low female participation in the market economy is reflected in low public transfers in the form of pensions during the mature years and men's consequent cash transfers to women within the family.

Table 4.3 Sources for financing consumption during young ages with an LCD

Finance of consumption	LCD young ages					
	0	1–3	4–5	6–14	15–26	Total
Total	**100.0**	**100.0**	**100.0**	**100.0**	**100.0**	**100.0**
Production	**0.0**	**0.0**	**3.0**	**5.4**	**48.7**	**24.4**
Market	*0.0*	*0.0*	*0.0*	*0.0*	*33.0*	*15.2*
Non-market	*0.0*	*0.0*	*3.0*	*5.4*	*15.7*	*9.2*
Private transfers	**77.6**	**80.8**	**67.0**	**59.6**	**37.7**	**52.9**
Market	*24.2*	*30.6*	*33.3*	*38.8*	*31.5*	*33.7*
Non-market	*53.4*	*50.2*	*33.7*	*20.8*	*6.2*	*19.2*
Public transfers	**21.5**	**18.5**	**29.7**	**34.7**	**6.3**	**19.1**
Asset-based Reallocation	**0.9**	**0.7**	**0.3**	**0.3**	**7.3**	**3.6**

Source Author's elaborations on Eurostat (2008c, d), Istat (2008b; 2009), Banca d'Italia (2008) and various other sources

Table 4.4 Sources for financing consumption during mature ages with an LCD

Finance of consumption	LCD mature ages					
	59–64	65–69	70–74	75–79	80+	Total
Production	***78.9***	***52.4***	***44.0***	***38.5***	***26.8***	***50.2***
Market	*38.1*	*11.5*	*4.8*	*2.7*	*1.0*	*13.5*
Non-market	*40.8*	*40.9*	*39.2*	*35.8*	*25.8*	*36.7*
Private transfers	**−8.3**	**−5.7**	**−5.6**	**−5.5**	**−1.0**	**−5.3**
Market	*−2.8*	*−1.5*	*−3.0*	*−4.5*	*−4.2*	*−3.1*
Non-market	*−5.5*	*−4.2*	*−2.6*	*−1.0*	*3.2*	*−2.2*
Public transfers	**8.6**	**33.1**	**42.0**	**50.3**	**70.4**	**38.7**
Asset-based Reallocation	**20.8**	**20.2**	**19.6**	**16.7**	**3.8**	**16.4**
Total	**100.0**	**100.0**	**100.0**	**100.0**	**100.0**	**100.0**

Source Author's elaborations on Eurostat (2008c, d), Istat (2008b; 2009), Banca d'Italia (2008) and various other sources

Tables 4.3 and 4.4 provide a final overview of financing consumption by economic activity and sector for young and mature ages with economic deficits. The deficit age groups are further disaggregated in order to obtain a more detailed picture of the intergenerational reallocation system.

Children up to age 14 depend on transfers to finance their consumption, whereas starting from age 15 production is the main source of financing. However, both the kind (public or private) and the form (cash or time) of transfers vary considerably with age. Familial transfers provide for almost 80% of the consumption of children up to three years of age, the majority of which occur in the form of time. Nevertheless, it is possible to observe important differences even in the earliest years of the life course. First, time transfers are particularly relevant for newborns due to the intrinsic nature of their needs. Second, public transfers provide for a higher proportion of newborns' consumption than they do for toddlers (21.5 and

18.5%, respectively) due to public expenditures for birth and health care during the first year of life. The shares of time and cash transfers are balanced for children at kindergarten ages, at which point the share of familial transfers declines to 67.0%. Cash transfers represent the greatest amount of private transfers (38.8%) and public transfers contribute to a larger proportion to children's consumption (34.7%) during the compulsory schooling years. Finally, children aged from 15 to 26 years are able to finance almost half of their consumption through their production (48.7%, of which 33% is constituted by labor income and the remaining 15.7% by unpaid domestic work). Additionally, asset-based reallocations become more relevant (7.3%), most likely because market work allows adult children to accumulate small amounts of savings and assets. By contrast, the contribution of public transfers is significantly lower for this age group (6.3%). The limited participation of the state in financing consumption for children after mandatory school ages is reflected in a relatively high contribution by families (37.7%).

Production is an important source of financing consumption during the mature years (Table 4.3). However, on average, production is the main source of financing through age 69. Production provides for 78.9% of consumption until age 64, with the share dropping to 52.4% for the subsequent age group, which has reached the minimum legal age for retirement (65). This is also visible in the changing composition of production; labor income represents 38.1 and 11.5% of production for the age groups 60–64 and 65–69, respectively. Non-market production also remains relevant at subsequent ages, providing for 35.8 and 25.8% of consumption for the age groups 70–79 and 80 and above, respectively. As the role of production in financing consumption weakens, that of public transfers becomes increasingly significant, due mostly to pensions. Interestingly, private transfers are negative at all ages, meaning that people provide transfers to other family members rather than receive transfers to finance their own consumption. It should be noted that both private cash and time transfers are negative with the exception of the very oldest age group, at which time transfers are positive; those 80 and above receive time transfers in order to meet their domestic needs. Finally, asset-based reallocations provide for approximately 20.8% of consumption from ages 59 to 64, decrease to 16.7% from ages 75 to 79, and account for only 3.8% of consumption from age 80 onward. The decreasing trend with age of asset-based reallocation suggests that people accumulate savings and assets to finance consumption during retirement ages and, as they age, the relevance of asset-based reallocations declines as they are used up. After retirement, people typically tend to use savings to purchase a new house, a new car, or anything that can be seen as a personal reward for the long years spent working in the market. In addition to this phenomenon, strategies of saving and investment are forward-looking behaviors (Sanderson and Scherbov 2007), so people are less likely to use their savings or sell assets at older ages as their life expectancy involves fewer remaining years.

4.9 Concluding Remarks

This chapter extends the NTA research on the economic lifecycle and intergenerational support system in order to disaggregate in greater detail the age-specific measures of SNA economic activities by gender and to include nonmonetary transfers in the analysis of the intergenerational support system. The results make abundantly clear that considering only market activities leads to an incomplete or even misleading picture of the real relations in the economy and in the intergenerational support system.

Not surprisingly, the nationwide picture of the gender- and age-specific economic lifecycle and age reallocations for Italy in 2008 show that men generated more labor income for more years than women. Within the market, women are barely able to finance their own consumption by means of their own labor from ages 37 to 55, whereas men generate a considerable LCS between ages 25 and 60. As a result, men redistribute resources within the family not only to children but also to women. However, the inclusion of the non-market economy reveals the existence of a dramatically different reality. Even at young ages, female children contribute more to household production than male children. From age 20 and throughout their remaining lives, women produce more unpaid domestic services and goods than they consume, while men consume more domestic time then they produce during the entire life course. The results of the analysis of Italy in 2008 make it possible to assert with confidence the existence of a reverse gender pattern of production and transfers between the market economy and the non-market economy. Nevertheless, women have a market surplus that allows them to supply their own consumption for a meaningful period of their lives, while men depend upon women to provide for their non-market consumption during the entire course of their lives.

Results for the total economy show that the inclusion of the non-market-economy extends the age production border to a significantly later point in life, raises the value of the LCD among the young and the value of the LCS in the middle years, and decreases the economic dependence of those in the mature age groups, although the latter two effects are due entirely to the age patterns of the non-market production of women. Familial transfers represent more than 50% of the total transfers received by dependent children in the total economy. The share of private transfers reaches 80% for children aged 0–3 years, when the great majority of transfers occur in the form of time provided mostly by women.

In summary, the results of this chapter clearly demonstrate that the generational contract in Italy depends on a gender contract; men's financial transfers to dependent age groups are made possible to a significant degree by women's time transfers within the family. The combination of paid and unpaid work for women in the middle stages of life raises concerns about the equity and sustainability of the gender contract. Public care provision for children at young ages, especially nursery service, represents a key area of intervention to lighten the intergenerational obligations burden on women.

References

Anxo, D., Mencarini, A., Pailhé, A., Solaz, A., Tanturri, M. L., & Flood, L. (2007). Gender differences in time use over the life course in France, Italy, Sweden, and the US. *Feminist Economics, 17*(3), 159–195.

Apps, P., & Rees, P. (2005). Gender, time use, and public policy over the life cycle. *Oxford Review of Economic Policy, 21*(3), 439–461.

Donehower, G. (2014). Incorporating gender and time use into NTA: National Time Transfer Accounts methodology. http://www.ntaccounts.org/doc/repository/Incorporating%20Gender%20and%20Time%20Use%20into%20NTA,%20Version%203.docx. Accessed December 3, 2016.

Donehower, G., & Mejia-Guevara, I. (2012). *Everybody works: Gender, age and economic activity*. Paper presented at the 2012 Meeting of the Population Association of America, San Francisco, 3–5 May 2012.

Eurostat. (2004). Guidelines on harmonised European time use surveys. Luxembourg: Eurostat. https://www.h5.scb.se/tus/tus/doc/KS-CC-04-007-EN.pdf. Accessed December 28, 2016.

Eurostat. (2009). Harmonised European time use surveys—2008 guidelines. Retrieved from Luxembourg: http://ec.europa.eu/eurostat/ramon/statmanuals/files/KS-RA-08-014-EN.pdf. Accessed December 28, 2016.

Eurostat. (2014). Population and social conditions. Available at http://epp.eurostat.ec.europa.eu/portal/page/portal/statistics/search_database. Accessed December 28, 2016.

Fisher, K. (2015). Metadata of time use studies. Last updated December 31, 2014. Centre for Time Use Research, University of Oxford, United Kingdom. http://www.timeuse.org/information/studies/. Accessed December 28, 2016.

Friedman, J. H. (1984). SMART user's guide: Technical Report No. 1. Department of Statistics, Stanford University. https://statistics.stanford.edu/sites/default/files/LCS%2001.pdf. Accessed December 28, 2016.

Hammer, B., Prskawetz, A., & Freund, I. (2015). Production activities and economic dependency by age and gender in Europe: A cross-country comparison. *The Journal of the Economics of Ageing, 5,* 86–97.

Gershuny, J., & Fisher K. (2013). Multinational Time Use Study. Centre for Time Use Research, University of Oxford

Lee, R., & Lapkoff, S. (1988). Intergenerational flows of time and goods, and consequences of slowing population growth. *Journal of Political Economy, 96*(3), 618–651.

Phananiramai, M. (2011). Incorporating time into the National Transfer Accounts: The case of Thailand. In R. Lee & A. Mason (Eds.), *Population aging and the generational economy: A global perspective* (pp. 528–541). Northampton, MA: Edward Elgar Publishing.

Reid, M. (1934). *Economics of household production*. New York: Wiley.

Sanderson, W. C., & Scherbov, S. (2007). A new perspective on population aging. *Demographic Research, 16*(2), 27–58.

Szalai, A. (1966). The multinational comparative time budget research project: A venture in international research cooperation. *American Behavioral Scientist, 10*(4), 1–31.

Vargha, L., Šeme, A., Gál, R. I., Hammer, B., & Sambt, J. (2016). European National Time Transfer Accounts. Available at: http://witt.null2.net/shiny/agenta/. Accessed on December 28, 2016.

Vargha, L, Gál, R.I., & Crosby-Nagy, M. O. (2017) Household production and consumption over the lifecycle: National Time Transfer Accounts in 14 European countries. *Demographic Research*, 36(32), 905–944.

Zagheni, E., & Zannella, M. (2013). The life cycle dimension of time transfers in Europe. *Demographic Research, 29*(35), 937–948.

Zagheni, E., Zannella, M., Movsesyan, G., & Wagner, B. (2015). *A comparative analysis of European time transfers between generations and genders*. Heidelberg: Springer.

Statistical Sources

Banca d'Italia. (2008). Indagine sui bilanci delle famiglie italiane.
Eurostat. (2008a). Annual sector accounts. http://ec.europa.eu/eurostat/web/sector-accounts/data/database. Accessed December 28, 2016.
Eurostat. (2008b). Government finance statistics, annual government statistics, final consumption expenditure of households by consumption purpose (COICOP). https://data.europa.eu/euodp/it/data/dataset/E3td1eJcpRfbHOtLntXwA. Accessed December 28, 2016.
Eurostat. (2008c). Government finance statistics, annual government statistics, general government expenditure by function (COFOG). http://appsso.eurostat.ec.europa.eu/nui/show.do?dataset=gov_a_exp&lang=en. Accessed December 28, 2016.
Eurostat. (2008d). European system of integrated social protection statistics (ESSPROS). http://ec.europa.eu/eurostat/statistics-explained/index.php/Social_protection_statistics. Accessed December 28, 2016.
Istat. (2008a). Indagine sui consumi delle famiglie.
Istat. (2008b). Multiscopo sulle famiglie: uso del tempo.
Istat. (2009). Indagine sulle condizioni di vita.

Concluding Remarks

This research stems from the premise that the specter of aging societies calls for further advancements in statistical information and especially for the development of social welfare and age-related measures in public accounting. The National Transfer Accounts (NTA) project has developed an international standard to establish age-specific national accounts and measure comprehensively intergenerational exchanges in the economy.

In this monograph, an NTA is developed for Italy with reference to 2008. Following a recent development in the NTA approach, age-specific measures of economic activities and exchanges have been extended to include both the gendered and non-market dimensions of the total economy. This choice was motivated by the strong belief that household servicing represents a powerful argument for going beyond the traditional emphasis of welfare literature on cash transfers and that societal equity should be analyzed not only between generations, as proposed in the original debate on intergenerational conflicts and contracts, but also between genders.

The empirical analysis of the Italian intergenerational and gender support system revealed substantive results. First, the age-specific borders of economic dependence are significantly different than those conventionally adopted by demographic indicators. Children are economically dependent up to age 26, whereas later-life dependency begins at age 59. Comparisons with similar studies have revealed that economic dependence lasts longer in youth and starts earlier at mature ages in Italy than in other European countries. The inclusion of the non-market economy raises the value of children's LCDs but decreases that of the mature age groups, due to their prolonged activity in the household economy.

Second, the empirical results demonstrated the existence of a twofold direction of transfers; resources flow not only across generations but also between genders. The results showed the existence of a reverse gender pattern of the economic life cycle in the market and non-market economy. Within the market, on average, women are barely able to finance their own consumption by means of their own labor from ages 37 to 55, whereas men generate a considerable LCS between ages 25 and 60. As a result, men redistribute monetary resources within the family not only to children but also to women. However, the inclusion of the non-market

M. Zannella, *The Economic Lifecycle, Gender and Intergenerational Support*, SpringerBriefs in Population Studies, DOI 10.1007/978-3-319-62669-7

economy reveals the existence of a dramatically different situation. Even at young ages, female children contribute more to household production than male children. Beginning at age 20 and for the remainder of their lives, women provide time transfers to children and men. Interestingly, men consume more domestic time then they produce during all stages of life, meaning that they are always dependent, to a greater or lesser degree, on the household economy.

Finally, results from the social welfare perspective show that formal social protection provided by the state constitutes only the visible but hardly the most important part of the complex reality of the Italian intergenerational support system. The family has been shown to be at minimum an equally and likely more important institution than the state in the provision of welfare in Italy. In particular, the family appears to provide mechanisms that compensate for gaps in formal social protection, as demonstrated by the results confirming the existence of the strongly downward and upward directions of public and private transfers, respectively. The detailed analysis of public transfers provides empirical confirmation of the double-biased nature of the Italian welfare system; not only is formal welfare provision significantly unbalanced toward old age pensions but also the social needs of the working-age adults who sustain most of the fiscal burden are largely ignored. Those in the middle years of the life course are shown to be economically squeezed; they redistribute large amounts of resources not only within the state but also within the household. Meanwhile, generous pensions programs allow their recipients to redistribute financial resources within the family, which is considered a perverse redistributive paradox of the Italian welfare system.

Families are the main source of intergenerational support for dependent children; the amount of private transfers is significantly higher than public transfers for all deficit ages among youth. All in all, familial transfers contribute to finance more than 50% of children's deficit. The share increases to almost 80% for toddlers, of which more than 50% is in the form of time for care, most of which is provided by women. Family contributions decline in relative terms during the schooling years, with the market component becoming more relevant. By contrast, the slight participation of the state in financing the deficit of children after mandatory school ages is reflected in increasing family transfers.

This research has shed ample light on the complex nature of the Italian intergenerational support system by quantifying the size of public and family contributions to welfare along the life course. The research has also highlighted that analysis focused solely on the market economy provides an incomplete and seriously misleading picture of intergenerational and gender relations. The NTA, by providing innovative and detailed data, on age- and gender-specific economic activities and exchanges, represents an invaluable instrument for researcher and policymakers. The systematic development of NTA would significantly help the evaluation of institutions providing intergenerational support. New lines of research in the NTA project should include detailed analysis to account for the main sources of population heterogeneity and integration with well-being indicators.

FSC
www.fsc.org
MIX
Papier | Fördert
gute Waldnutzung
FSC® C083411

Kolibri 360 GmbH
Ferdinand-Jühlke-Straße 7
99095 Erfurt, Deutschland
produktsicherheit@kolibri360.de